Decorative
Painting 1-2-3®

Meredith® BOOKS

Decorative Painting 1-2-3®
Senior Editor: Vicki L. Ingham
Project Manager: Cathy Long
Copy Chief: Terri Fredrickson
Publishing Operations Manager: Karen Schirm
Senior Editor, Asset and Information Manager: Phillip Morgan
Edit and Design Coordinator: Mary Lee Gavin
Editorial and Design Assistant: Renee E. McAtee
Book Production Managers: Pam Kvitne, Marjorie J. Schenkelberg,
     Rick von Holdt, Mark Weaver
Contributing Copy Editor: Ira Lacher
Contributing Proofreaders: Jeanette Astor, Cheri Madison, Paula Reece
Indexer: Sharon Duffy
Graphic Designers: Tim Abramowitz, Joel Wires, Abramowitz
     Creative Studios
Photography: Marty Baldwin, Scott Little, Blaine Moats, Jason Wilde
Contributing Decorative Painters: Zachary Bunkers, Patricia Mohr
     Kramer, Molly Spain
Photostylists: Cathy Kramer, Molly Sinnett

Meredith® **Books**
Executive Director, Editorial: Gregory H. Kayko
Executive Director, Design: Matt Strelecki
Managing Editor: Amy Tincher-Durik
Executive Editor: Benjamin W. Allen
Senior Associate Design Director: Tom Wegner
Marketing Product Manager: Isaac Petersen

Publisher and Editor in Chief: James D. Blume
Editorial Director: Linda Raglan Cunningham
Executive Director, New Business Development: Todd M. Davis
Director, Sales—Home Depot: Robb Morris
Executive Director, Sales: Ken Zagor
Director, Operations: George A. Susral
Director, Production: Douglas M. Johnston
Director, Marketing: Amy Nichols
Business Director: Jim Leonard

Vice President and General Manager: Douglas J. Guendel

Meredith Publishing Group
President: Jack Griffin
Senior Vice President: Bob Mate

Meredith Corporation
Chairman and Chief Executive Officer: William T. Kerr
President and Chief Operating Officer: Stephen M. Lacy

In Memoriam: E.T. Meredith III (1933-2003)

The Home Depot®
Marketing Manager: Tom Sattler
© Copyright 2005 by Homer TLC, Inc. Second Edition.
All rights reserved. Printed in the United States of America.
Library of Congress Control Number: 2005928621
ISBN: 0-696-22248-5
The Home Depot® and **1-2-3**® are registered trademarks of Homer
TLC, Inc.

Distributed by Meredith Corporation.
Meredith Corporation is not affiliated with The Home Depot®.

We are dedicated to providing accurate and helpful do-it-yourself
information. We welcome your comments about improving this book and
ideas for other books we might offer to home improvement enthusiasts.

Contact us by any of these methods:
Leave a voice message at: 800/678-2093
Write to: Meredith Books, Home Depot Books
     1716 Locust St.
     Des Moines, IA 50309–3023
Send e-mail to: hi123@mdp.com.

How to use this book

Painting is the fastest and easiest way to transform your rooms. A coat of fresh color on the walls breathes life into any space—and decorative paint techniques go a step further, adding dimension, drama, and distinctive personality. Decorative painting includes three types of finishes: faux (French for "false") effects that make surfaces look like something they're not—leather, stone, denim, or aged plaster, for example; methods of application that add depth, texture, or pattern, such as sponging with a glaze mixture or applying paint in stripes, blocks, or diamonds; and stencils, which let you create a repeating pattern with a template. Techniques can be combined—sponging, striping, and stenciling, for example—for one-of-a-kind decorating solutions. In the pages that follow, you'll find detailed instructions for some of the most popular techniques as well as some new ones.

To help you plan, prepare, and paint, this book is divided into the following sections:

Tool time

The right tools and materials make all the difference for any project. This chapter introduces supplies and equipment that will help make your painting project both efficient and successful. You'll find general information about paints and sheens as well as a chart to help you estimate how much paint you will need to complete your project. A visual guide to basic painting and decorative painting tools helps you know what to look for when you shop for supplies. And you'll learn when it's better to use a brush than a roller.

It's all about color

Color is key to your room's personality, and combining new colors and decorative techniques will make your home come alive. This chapter defines terms you'll need to know and offers information on the effect of lighting on color. You'll also learn how to use paint chips to select color and how to use glaze medium.

Preparation is key

Don't skip this step! Success for any painting project results from careful planning and solid preparation before applying that first coat of paint. In fact, 80 percent of the time spent on your project will be devoted to preparing the surfaces for the final finish. The entire process is outlined in this chapter with detailed step-by-step instructions for repairing and smoothing your walls, applying the right primers and sealers, and applying the base coat of paint.

Decorative painting

This chapter provides step-by-step instructions for 40 popular decorative paint finishes. Look under each technique for the tools and materials you'll need and the estimated amount of time to apply the technique in a 12-foot-square room with 8-foot ceilings. The paint colors you'll need are listed by color name and shown in paint swatches at the bottom of the page. Turn to the Resources section to find the brand name and number for each color. Also note the "Before You Begin" box: Here you'll find instructions for base-coating and any other steps required before starting the decorative technique itself.

Keep it clean

It's not the fun part, but good cleanup practices pay off in the long run. Learn how to care for brushes and rollers and seal leftover paint, as well as how to dispose of empty paint cans, contaminated solvents, and dirty rags in an environmentally safe manner.

Resources

Look here to find the brand name and complete paint identification information for each color used in the techniques.

Decorative Painting 1-2-3.

Table of contents

Chapter 1
TOOLS AND MATERIALS 6

Chapter 2
CHOOSING COLORS 20

Chapter 3
ROOM PAINTING BASICS 36

Chapter 4

DECORATIVE TECHNIQUES 54

Chapter 5

CLEANING UP 174

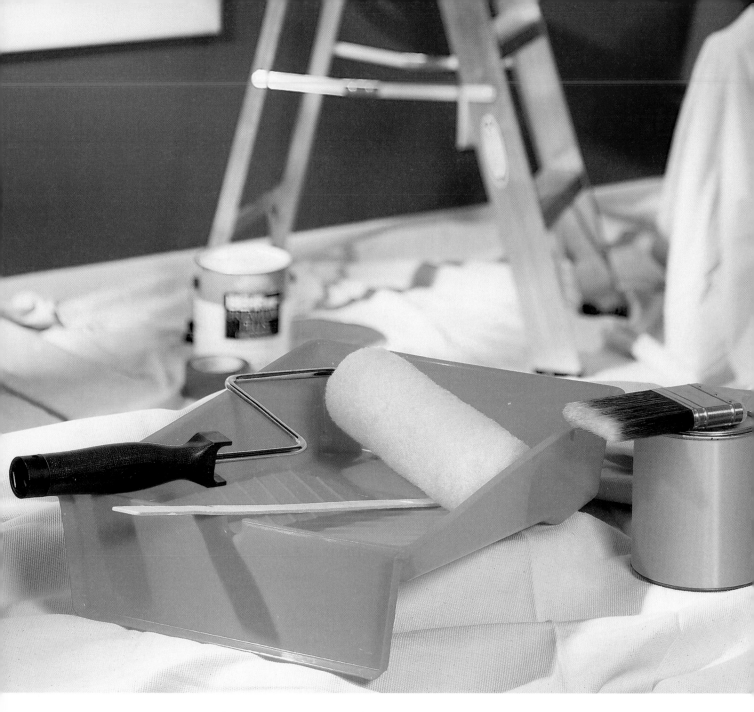

Tools and materials

quipping yourself with the proper painting gear will save time and effort. Quality tools and materials are an investment in painting success—starting with the right paint. Read on for complete information on selecting the best type of paint, sheen options, and estimating the correct amount of paint for each job. There is an overview of the tools every painter should have on hand for both wall preparation and basic painting. Decorative painting techniques often call for specialty tools; if a project you want to try calls for a tool you're not familiar with, check the chart on page 15 to see what it looks like. Basic painting always starts with the right brush. A quality brush is worth its weight in gold and is one of the best investments a painter can make. Good brushes hold more paint, provide better coverage, and if

Chapter 1 highlights

properly cared for, will last for years. For large, flat areas, a paint roller is best. Investing in a good quality roller pays off with swift, even paint application. Inexpensive roller covers are fine for small jobs, but if you enjoy redecorating, you'll want to invest in high-quality covers that you can use over and over. See pages 18 and 19 to learn what to look for.

Safety considerations

LEAD PAINT ALERT

If you are sanding or removing paint, especially if it is light-colored and applied before 1978 (it may be hidden beneath one or more top coats), have it tested for lead by a professional (or use a household lead test kit from The Home Depot). Do not attempt to remove lead-based paint either by sanding or with a heat gun. Contact the Environmental Protection Agency (EPA) at 800-424-LEAD or www.epa.gov/lead for guidance.

Think safety when you paint and protect yourself as carefully as you do your possessions.

Painting safety starts by taking care of yourself. When you're painting inside, keep these critical points of protection in mind:

■ **Eyes.** When you are scraping, power sanding, painting overhead, or spray-painting, wear plastic safety glasses or goggles to protect your eyes from flying particles and paint droplets. If you get something in your eye, rinse it out immediately with fresh water.

■ **Hands.** Many liquids associated with painting (thinners, removers, cleaning solvents, and bleach) are toxic or harmful to your skin. When handling these liquids, wear appropriate gloves: latex for latex paints and stains, neoprene for most solvents. Wear cloth work gloves when sanding, scraping, or using cleaning pads, such as steel wool.

■ **Feet.** Paints are slippery liquids. Wear shoes with slip-resistant soles.

■ **Lungs.** Two things to keep out of your lungs are solids and solvents. Paint projects generate both. Sanding produces a fine powder, which is difficult to avoid breathing. The most dangerous dust is that from lead-based paint or from asbestos in older ceiling tiles that were installed before 1978. If you suspect lead (any paint purchased or applied before 1978), have it tested (look for household lead test kits at your home improvement center; also see "Safety Alert," above left); if it is lead-based paint, do not sand it. When sanding paint that is not lead-based, wear a tight-fitting, dust-resistant mask.

When you smell a solvent or paint, you are breathing it. Wear a respirator recommended for the solvent and be sure the space is adequately ventilated whenever you are working indoors.

■ **Clothing.** Wear an old, loose-fitting shirt and pants. Put on an inexpensive, lightweight painter's cap to keep paint spatter out of your hair.

Safety precautions

There are several phases of any painting project that require safety precautions and the right equipment for the job:

■ **Scraping, sanding, and wire brushing.** Protect your eyes from flying particles by wearing plastic goggles. Wear gloves to protect your hands from sharp scrapers and wire brushes. Protect your lungs from sanding dust by wearing a tight-fitting, dust-resistant mask.

■ **Removing paint with chemical strippers or a heat gun.** For furniture projects, work outdoors whenever possible. When painting rooms, provide plenty of ventilation by opening windows on at least two walls and using a fan. Always wear a chemical fumes respirator. Protect your hands with neoprene gloves. Keep children and pets out of range of the dangerous solvents and fumes.

■ **Using stepladders.** Make sure the stepladder contacts the floor solidly on all four feet, or it may move unexpectedly. Before you stand on it, lock the ladder in the open position by pushing down on the braces until they catch. Never try to shift a stepladder while standing on it. Don't ever stand on the top two steps; if you can't easily reach what you're trying to paint, you need a taller ladder.

■ **Applying paint.** Protect your eyes with goggles when you're painting overhead or using a paint sprayer. When you use a sprayer, double-check hoses and fittings and check the spray in a safe direction. Wear a respirator when you use solvent-based paint and turn off all pilot lights and other spark sources. To avoid spills, place open paint containers where you won't trip over them; keep children and pets away from the area. Wear shoes with slip-resistant soles.

■ **Storing paints and solvents.** Make sure paint containers are unbreakable and securely sealed with childproof lids. To reduce paint skinning to an absolute minimum, store the can upside down.

■ **Disposing of paints and stains.** Never dispose of liquid paint or stain with ordinary household trash. Instead, try to use leftover material by applying another coat. In some locations it is permissible to place empty or thoroughly solidified cans in the trash. Call 800-CLEANUP or check with your local trash department for your state or county regulations. If permissible, paint can be dried by pouring paint hardener, vermiculite, or cat litter into the can and leaving the lid off until the mass solidifies. Place the can in a secure location while it dries out.

■ **Always use adequate ventilation.** When you're working with solvents, thinners, paint particles, or dust from sanding and finishing, wear the correct respirator or mask for the project. Open windows and doors to provide adequate ventilation and to remove toxic vapors and particles from the work area.

Safety equipment

You are vulnerable to particles and fumes when you are sanding, painting, or working with solvents.

To protect your skin:

- Wear cotton gloves when using sharp or abrasive tools.
- Wear latex gloves when painting with latex paint.
- Wear neoprene gloves when handling solvents, strippers, and harsh chemicals.

Neoprene gloves

To protect your eyes:

- Wear safety glasses when working with tools.
- Wear goggles to protect against dust and aerosol droplets when sanding, spraying, or painting over your head.

Safety goggles

To protect your lungs:

- Sand, paint, and strip outside, or cross-ventilate with at least two open windows or doors.
- If there is a danger of breathing dust, aerosols, or solvent fumes, filter the air with a respirator. Check product labels for the recommended respirator.

Respirators are of two types

Particulate respirators (dust-resistant masks) filter out dry particles and most non-oil-based liquid droplets. Use a particulate respirator when sanding bare or painted wood (except lead-based paint), drywall, and rusted surfaces. Special-purpose particulate respirators are available for spraying latex paint and sanding (not burning) lead-based paint.

Sanding mask

Latex mask

Lead mask

Cartridge respirators contain both particulate filters and chemically active canisters for absorbing solvent vapors. Use a cartridge respirator when spraying solvent-based paints and working with solvents and strippers.

Note: Unless specifically stated otherwise, no homeowner-type respirator protects against lead fumes, asbestos fibers, or sandblasting.

Fitting respirators

A respirator must form an airtight seal around nose and mouth. Respirators don't work with beards. To fit a particulate respirator:

Cartridge respirator

- Position the mask under your chin.
- Pull the top and bottom straps over your head and position them just above and below your ears.
- Using the same fingers of both hands, mold the soft metal nose strap to your nose.
- Test the fit by covering the mask with both hands and drawing a sharp breath; it should be difficult to breathe.

To fit a cartridge respirator:

- Place the respirator loosely over your face, low on the bridge of your nose.
- Fasten the straps for a snug but comfortable fit.
- Test the fit by covering the air inlets and breathing in gently. The mask should draw up against your face, and you should neither hear nor feel any leakage. If you smell fumes or feel dizzy, either the respirator doesn't fit, the canisters are the wrong type, or they are used up.

Always read the warnings on paint, solvent, and stripper containers, and compare them to the listed capabilities of the respirator canister.

Follow these tips to work safely. It's the most important part of any home improvement project.

Select the right paint

There are two ways to define quality when it comes to paint. Every painting expert will tell you to buy quality (meaning good) paint. Quality paint provides better coverage, truer color, and requires less work to apply. But the word "quality" appears on almost every can of paint in the store, and labels don't really help define what makes a good paint. So how do you know you are getting a good product? The simple answer is price. Generally, the more you pay, the better-quality paint you get.

But there's another quality consideration as well. What do you need to do the job? People paint for different reasons. A family with kids who like to draw on the walls needs a paint that is durable and washable. A short-term renter is looking for low cost. A contractor wants a paint that is inexpensive and hides well. A decorator is looking for intensity and range of color. Let the people at your paint center help you decide what level of quality is right for you.

Choosing paint involves more than picking a color. Understand the basics to make the best selection.

Latex or oil?

Latex paints have several advantages over alkyds (oils). Latex is flexible, thins and cleans up with water, dries quickly, and has nontoxic fumes. In exterior applications its ability to breathe water vapor reduces peeling and blistering.

Alkyds have greater adhesion over smooth, nonabsorbent surfaces, such as plastics and metals. And they can hold a greater percentage of solids (ground pigments), often allowing single-coat coverage.

Sometimes the best solution is both: an alkyd primer for adhesion and hiding, followed by a latex top coat. The question of which to choose may soon be academic, as the Environmental Protection Agency (EPA) and state authorities are increasingly limiting the use of alkyd (solvent-based) paints.

Latex and oil (alkyd) paints compared

PAINT TYPE	GENERAL ADVANTAGES	GENERAL LIMITATIONS
Latex	■ cleans up with water ■ excellent color and gloss retention ■ good adhesion to many surfaces ■ breathes (allows moisture vapor to pass)	■ most can't be applied below 50°F ■ liquid paint may be ruined by freezing
Alkyd	■ good hiding ability ■ high adhesion ■ allows longer time to brush ■ good flow-out of brush marks ■ resistance to sticking (blocking)	■ flammability ■ yellows, embrittles, cracks with age ■ not for use on galvanized metal or fresh masonry ■ high volatile organic compound (VOC) content and resulting odor

Sheens

Once you've chosen between oil and latex and once you've chosen your color, you still have at least five different sheens to choose from—flat, eggshell, satin, semigloss, and gloss. Each is a measure of how much light the paint reflects. A flat paint reflects perhaps 5 to 10 percent of the light that shines on it; a gloss reflects 50 percent of the light or more. With changes in sheen come changes in the appearance of both the surface and the color. A flat sheen looks duller and darker than the same color in a gloss.

Paint manufacturers continue to develop and improve on paint formulations. In addition to the five standard sheens, some companies are offering a flat latex enamel and a sateen finish. The flat enamel is scrubbable thanks to a harder finish than standard flat-sheen paints. The sateen finish is low-luster and designed esepcially for kitchens and baths.

Paint sheen

SHEEN	BEST FOR	BENEFITS
Flat	■ walls and ceilings (except kitchen/bath)	■ muted appearance ■ hides imperfections
Eggshell	■ walls and ceilings (can be used in kitchen/bath)	■ best touch-up characteristics ■ better dirt resistance (eggshell)
Satin	■ walls in any room ■ kitchen and bath ceilings	■ resists dirt better than flat ■ richer in appearance than flat
Semigloss	■ high-traffic area walls (kitchens, baths) ■ doors, trim, shelving	■ resists dirt and easily cleaned ■ not as shiny as gloss
Gloss	■ doors, trim, shelving, kitchen cabinets, bathrooms, and wet rooms	■ resists dirt and mildew ■ easily cleaned ■ best water resistance ■ reflective—bright appearance

Paint sheen comparison

FLAT

Flat paint absorbs light and therefore hides many surface imperfections. Dents, dings, changes in texture, and undulations in the surface all tend to disappear behind the matte finish of a flat paint. Because it hides blemishes so well, you can often apply a single coat. On the down side, it tends to show dirt and doesn't stand up well to scrubbing.

EGGSHELL

Eggshell hides many imperfections but is a bit smoother than flat, meaning it reflects more light. It's also easier to wash and therefore more durable. Because of its washability, it has become a popular sheen for walls.

SATIN

Think washability when you think satin—kitchens, bathrooms, hallways, kids' rooms, woodwork, and trim. Satin paint's silky finish looks good on walls and is smooth enough to stand up to dirt and cleaning.

SEMIGLOSS

Semigloss is synonymous with shiny washability. Semigloss reflects between 35 and 50 percent of the light that hits it, and most people find it too shiny on walls. It's extremely durable, however, and well suited to surfaces that get a lot of handprints—trim, woodwork, cabinets, and doors. For the same reason, it's also popular in kitchens and baths.

GLOSS

For utility room or playroom walls, and for trim that gets a lot of abuse, the easy cleanability of gloss is a good call. Used on walls, however, the high shine may be discomforting. Minor surface imperfections suddenly look like glaring errors.

Paint estimator

Walls

1 **CALCULATE THE WALL AREA**
Multiply the length of each wall by the height of the ceiling and add them up:

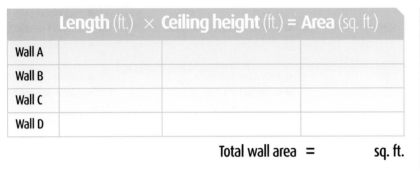

Length (ft.)	× Ceiling height (ft.)	= Area (sq. ft.)
Wall A		
Wall B		
Wall C		
Wall D		

Total wall area = _____ sq. ft.

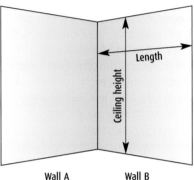

Wall A   Wall B

2 **CALCULATE THE QUANTITY OF PAINT NEEDED**
Divide the total wall area by 400 square feet per gallon to get the quantity of paint needed **per coat**. For rough or textured surfaces, divide by 300 square feet. Dark colors will need three or more coats, while lighter colors may need only two. When you're doing decorative techniques, these calculations will apply to the base-coat color only. See page 35 for guidelines on how much paint to buy for mixing with glazes. (Note: Coverage per gallon noted above is industry standard; check the paint label for specific information.)

	Total wall area (sq. ft.)	÷ Coverage (sq. ft./gallon)	= Paint needed (gallons)
Smooth surface		÷ 400	
Rough surface		÷ 300	

HOW ABOUT WINDOWS AND DOORS?
It usually isn't necessary to deduct the square footage taken up by windows and doors in the average wall when estimating how much paint is needed to do a room. An exception would be on walls with oversize windows or with several windows or doors.

Ceilings or floors

1 **CALCULATE THE SURFACE AREA**
Multiply the length by the width to get the surface area.
Length (ft.) × Width (ft.) = Surface area (sq. ft.)

2 **CALCULATE THE QUANTITY OF PAINT NEEDED**
Divide the surface area by the coverage per gallon to get the number of gallons needed. (See Step 2 above.)

	Total ceiling/floor area (sq. ft.)	÷ Coverage (sq. ft./gallon)	= Paint needed (gallons)
Smooth surface		÷ 400	
Rough surface		÷ 300	

Stepladders

A good stepladder provides the stability you need to paint out-of-reach areas. For ceilings 8 feet or lower, a 4-foot stepladder is adequate; in homes with higher ceilings, you'll need at least a 6-foot stepladder. Price is based on the materials used in the ladder's construction.

- Though expensive, fiberglass ladders are lightweight, strong, and do not conduct electricity.
- Aluminum is nearly as lightweight and strong, and about half the price of fiberglass.
- Wood is heaviest and the least expensive.

When you're shopping for a ladder, look for special features to make your job easier. For instance, some foldout shelves include a paper towel holder, tracks for hand tools, even a special paint bucket holder.

Regardless of the kind or size of ladder, follow the safety rules illustrated on this page.

BUILD A SCAFFOLD
Use two ladders and a plank to build a scaffold that is safe, convenient, and relatively easy to move. Snap the ladder's locking bars in place and set the plank on the steps. Never use the foldout shelf as a step.

SAFETY ALERT

Never stand on the top step of a ladder—not even just this once or for just a moment. Use a taller ladder if necessary to reach the highest points.

FOLLOW THE MANUFACTURER'S WEIGHT RATING
Never exceed the manufacturer's weight rating printed on the yellow sticker. And don't remove the sticker!

SNAP LOCKING BARS INTO POSITION
Make sure the locking bars are snapped in the locked position before setting in place and using the ladder.

WORK SMARTER

PLACE NEEDED EQUIPMENT ON THE FOLDOUT SHELF
Use the foldout shelf to hold your bucket or roller tray—not as a step. Don't even stand on the step opposite the shelf.

CREATE A PLANK TO REACH HIGH AREAS
To paint above a stairway, use a tall stepladder on the bottom stair landing and lay an aluminum telescoping plank from a stair tread to the ladder step that is closest to the same level. Firmly position the plank between the step and the ladder; wear slip-resistant shoes. Don't stand on the edge of the plank.

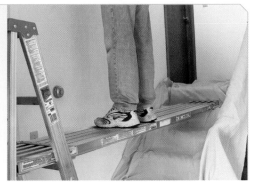

The painter's tool kit

G ood-quality tools are one of the most important investments you'll make as you become more involved in home improvement projects. The tools on this page will help you get the best painting results possible. Some you may already have and some you'll need to purchase. When you're preparing for a project, fill out your tool list with the best products you can afford. Good tools save you time and effort. If cared for properly, quality tools will last a long time and will make your painting experience easier. Good tools help guarantee great results.

5-GALLON BUCKET
Use if applying more than one gallon on a job. Ensures even mix of color and easy storage.

BRUSH AND ROLLER SPINNER
Used to clean roller covers and brushes.

SQUIRREL MIXER
Attaches to an electric drill. Ensures even mixing of paint.

POUR SPOUT FOR GALLON CAN
Fits in the paint can's rim. Eliminates drips and spills when pouring.

ROLLERS
Applicators made of synthetic or natural fiber of various thicknesses, or "nap," attached to a solid core.

THICK NAP ROLLER
The 1¼-inch-thick nap is ideal for rolling paint onto extra-rough surfaces.

1-QUART PAINT BUCKET
Pro-recommended alternative to painting straight from the can. A bucket is inexpensive and essential.

BRUSHES
Quality varies; choose the right brush for the job.

PAINT CAN OPENER
Designed not to damage rim of paint can when opening.

ROLLER GRID FOR 5-GALLON BUCKET
Allows clean and even loading of paint on roller when using a plastic 5-gallon bucket.

RUBBER SANDING BLOCK
For hand-sanding. The block holds sheets of sandpaper, is easy to grip, and conforms to slightly uneven surfaces.

STAINLESS WIRE BRUSH
For removing loose paint, dirt, and rust particles.

10-IN-1 TOOL
Cleans paint rollers, opens paint cans, pulls nails, opens bottles, spreads and scrapes.

CAULKING GUN
For applying caulk to holes and cracks.

PAINTER'S TAPE
Blue painter's tape is formulated for easy removal. Use brown tape to protect a larger area.

ROLLER PAN
Holds paint that will be applied with a roller. Look for sturdy construction with a deep well.

RAGS
Indispensable for cleaning up drips and spills.

TAPE MEASURE
For measuring areas to be painted and laying out decorative patterns.

3-INCH SCRAPER
For applying and smoothing spackle. Can also be used to remove wallpaper if the corners are rounded.

EXTENSION POLE
Holds paint roller; telescopes to allow easy and less taxing application of paint on ceilings and high walls. Comes in several lengths.

PLASTIC MISTING BOTTLE
Used for priming (dampening slightly) roller covers and brushes before applying latex paint.

ROLLER PAN LINER
Disposable container to hold paint in roller pan. Makes cleanup and multiple color use easier.

ROLLER CAGES
Buy good-quality cages that will hold the roller covers securely in place while painting.

PAINT PAD
Quickly applies paint to smooth and lightly textured surfaces. Use with all paints and stains.

Decorative painting tools

T hese tools allow you to create the various effects shown in Chapter 4. In some cases, the tools will simply make the job easier. Others are essential for producing the desired result.

2½-QUART CONTAINER WITH PRINTED MEASUREMENTS
For easy measuring of paint and glaze mixtures.

4-INCH AND 7-INCH MINI ROLLER PANS
Hold paint that will be applied using 4- and 6-inch mini rollers.

4-INCH AND 6-INCH MINI ROLLER COVERS
Perfect for applying glazes and painting tight areas.

4-INCH AND 6-INCH MINI ROLLER FRAMES
Hold the 4- and 6-inch mini roller covers securely in place.

LEVEL WITH PRINTED MEASUREMENTS
Lets you measure and mark accurate horizontal and vertical lines.

DENIM WEAVER BRUSH
Creates a crosshatch pattern for the denim finish when dragged through wet glaze.

4-INCH DENIM CHECK ROLLER
Used for the denim finish, the notched metal disks create a "worn" appearance when rolled through wet glaze.

7-INCH LINEN WEAVER BRUSH
Creates a woven pattern resembling linen fabric when dragged horizontally and vertically through wet glaze.

LONG-BRISTLED BRUSH
Creates fine lines for the strié technique when dragged vertically through wet glaze.

9-INCH SPECIALTY FINISH ROLLER
Rolls on a specially formulated paint that mimics the natural look of suede.

GLAZE MEDIUM
Mixes with paint for a translucent effect. Slows drying to allow time to apply decorative finishes.

SQUEEGEE
Creates a variety of patterns when notched with either scissors or a crafts knife.

ARTIST'S BRUSHES
Use for detail work, such as lines, shading, and highlights.

NATURAL SEA SPONGES
Creates a random pattern when applying or removing paint and glaze.

LINT-FREE COTTON CLOTHS
Apply and remove paint and glaze for more defined results.

CHEESECLOTH
Use for blending and removing glazes for softer results.

PLASTIC TROWELS
Use to deposit and blend paints and glazes to create the illusion of texture.

6-INCH METAL PLASTER KNIFE
This flexible knife can apply and spread joint compound and plaster in textured finishes.

STENCIL BRUSH
Use in a stippling motion to apply paint for stenciling techniques.

5-INCH WOOD GRAINING TOOL
Drag in a slow, rocking motion through wet glaze to create realistic wood grains.

LARGE AND SMALL METALLIC ROLLER FRAME AND COVER
For applying metallic paints to create a subtle texture.

PLASTIC DROP CLOTH, 1 MIL THICK
Cut into sections and use to remove wet glaze for the leather finish.

FITCH EDGE TOOL
Used to apply or remove glaze in tight spots such as corners, along the ceiling, and around trimwork.

THE WOOLIE™
Sheepskin-covered pad with plastic handle ideal for creating clouds and other faux effects.

STIPPLE BRUSH
Used to remove glaze for the antique leather technique.

Proper paintbrushes

A good paintbrush feels like a natural extension of your hand. Brushes come in various qualities and prices.

Quality speaks. Bristle brushes are more expensive. They have earned their popularity with their variety of uses, ease of cleaning, and reuse capabilities. There are two types of bristles:

- Natural (usually hog) for solvent-based finishes;
- Synthetic (nylon or polyester) for water-based finishes. Some can be used with oil-based finishes as well.

The bristle edge. Compared with rollers and pads, the advantages of bristle brushes include:

- Versatility
- Durability and reusability
- Ability to apply a heavier coat
- Fastest cleanup

On the other hand. The disadvantages to bristles are:

- Slower application than a roller or pad
- Brush marks (a function of quality and expertise)
- Skill required to cover large areas

For quick projects. The least expensive are disposable brushes. They provide quick application of materials that are difficult to clean up, such as contact cement and fiberglass resin. Use low-cost foam brushes to apply smooth finishes to small areas.

Brush selection, use, and care are as critical to your success at painting as surface preparation.

The right brush for the job speeds the painting process and ensures better results. A wooden handle absorbs moisture, making holding easier. A plastic handle will get slippery.

Why quality brushes cost more

	TOP QUALITY	VS.	DISPOSABLE
	Flagged (split) bristle ends for a smoother finish	**BRISTLES**	Unflagged bristle ends
	Multiple wood spacer plugs to create paint reservoirs between bristle rows	**DIVIDER**	Single wood spacer plug
	Reinforced, rustproof ferrule to hold bristles securely	**FERRULE**	Weak ferrule, allowing bristles to fall out more easily
	Tapered end for better control	**HANDLE**	Blunt end

What to look for in a quality brush

A bristle length that is twice the width of the brush

A definite flex and snapback when pushed against your palm

Angled sash brushes with bristles cut at an angle to make cutting in easier and to create a softer finish

Straight, smooth bristles that are tightly packed with no gaps (to hold more paint)

Shedding no more than three or four bristles when tugged

Flagged (split) and tipped (varying lengths) ends for a smooth finish

Different shapes for different strokes

Sash brushes are good for reaching into corners.

Square-end (flat) brushes are best for flat surfaces.

Match the brush width to the width of the object being painted.

Paint rollers

Paint rollers are two-piece tools: there is a handle with a wire cage and threaded base, and an interchangeable roller cover.

A long-term investment. The handle will last as long as you clean it, so invest in the best you can afford. Look for these features:
- A grip that molds to your hand.
- A heavy frame, with minimum flex under pressure.
- Nylon bearings that spin easily.
- A cage with at least five wires and an antislip device.

For the job at hand. Roller covers range in quality. Bargain roller covers with paper cores break down quickly and cannot be reused. Use them for small jobs. Look for these features in a high-quality roller cover:
- A resin tube that won't break down in water.
- Beveled ends to avoid leaving edge beads.
- Seams that cannot be felt through the nap.
- Heavy, uniform nap that sheds little lint.

When should you use a roller? The roller lays down paint at least three times faster than the largest brush, and a good roller with beveled ends leaves no roller or overlap marks. A roller is the tool of choice for large, flat areas, such as ceilings and walls.

When should you use a brush? Use it when you need to paint narrow strips or cut in (paint a sharp edge). A roller has soft ends, so it cannot lay a sharp line of paint. For these tasks there is no substitute for a good brush.

It takes two. Most jobs will require both a roller and a paintbrush. The key is to understand when to use each applicator, and to know how to use each one properly, including pouring out only as much paint as you are going to need for the job.

A paint roller offers faster and easier paint application than a brush. Select from a variety of handles and covers.

It takes practice and the proper technique. Follow the simple steps that start on page 50 and you'll soon be rolling paint like a pro.

The standard 9-inch roller with an extension handle is the best choice for walls and ceilings.

A 4- or 6-inch mini roller is useful in tight spaces, such as around windows and trimwork. The roller is lightweight and easy to use.

The foam "hot dog" roller lays an ultrasmooth finish on smooth, flat surfaces.

A better roller has a molded handle, nylon bearings, a rectangular frame of heavy wire, and a five-wire cage.

Roller naps

The roller nap is the fiber that applies the paint. Select a roller nap designed for the texture of the wall you plan to paint and the type of paint you plan to use. As with many things in life, you get what you pay for. A cheap roller has a cardboard core that quickly goes out of round and a nap that will soon come off on the surface. It costs a little more to get a roller with a fiber core and well-attached nap, but it's easy to clean and will last through several jobs.

Most naps are nylon, good for both latex and alkyd paint. Lamb's wool rollers are excellent for applying alkyd paint, but they tend to soften in water-based paints and are expensive.

Common nap lengths vary from 3/16 inch to 1 1/4 inches. The longer the nap fiber, the rougher the surface it will cover. Short naps apply a smoother coat of paint and are recommended for dark colors.

Use a roller cover with a long nap for rough surfaces, a short nap for smooth surfaces.

Choose your roller nap to match the project. The smoother or glossier the surface, the shorter the nap you should use.

TOOL SAVVY

A MULTIPURPOSE TOOL

Buy a 10-in-1 tool, if for nothing else, to use as a roller scraper. It saves paint, clears a roller of solids buildup, and speeds cleanup immensely.

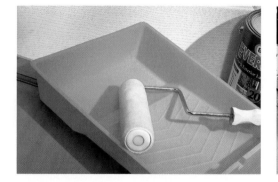

Use 3/16- and 1/4-inch naps with gloss paints on smooth surfaces, such as shelving and cabinets.

Use a 3/8-inch nap for flat and semigloss paint on walls and ceilings.

Use 1/2- and 3/4-inch naps for semirough surfaces, such as concrete floors and textured walls.

Use 1- or 1 1/4-inch naps for brick, concrete block, and heavy stucco or for applying metallic paints to walls.

Choosing colors

electing a color scheme is one of the first decisions you'll need to make before painting. This chapter describes the relationships between colors and explains how to design eye-pleasing color palettes. A good place to start is the color wheel. Made up of primary, secondary, and tertiary colors, the wheel shows how colors relate to each other. You can choose colors from one

side of the wheel for a harmonious blend or select two or three from opposite sides for a scheme based on contrast. Both approaches create satisfying combinations, and the scheme you settle on should reflect your personal tastes. This chapter also discusses the effects of light on color and how paint sheen can increase the brightness of a surface. Paint centers offer thousands of paint chips to aid in the selection of color, but before

Color can soothe or energize you. Learn how to harness its power to create the mood you want.

Chapter 2 highlights

KEY QUESTIONS
Ask yourself these questions to help guide your color selections.

22

THE COLOR WHEEL
Understanding this handy tool will help you see how colors work together so you can choose happy combinations.

23

HUE, INTENSITY, AND VALUE
These terms can help you communicate more clearly the effect you want to achieve.

25

BASIC COLOR SCHEMES
For a shortcut to success, pick one of these five tried-and-true formulas for assembling colors.

26

HOW LIGHT AFFECTS COLOR
Colors change dramatically under different types of light. Keep this in mind as you make selections.

29

COLOR MATCHING
Learn what color chips can and can't do for you.

33

USING GLAZES
Glazes are the decorative painter's best friend. Here are the basics for working with them.

35

applying paint to the wall, try out your colors by painting practice boards or test panels. These panels let you see how light affects the color during the day and in different parts of the room. Practice boards are also a good way to experiment with decorative paint techniques and see how glazes affect the color's appearance. Glaze, a milky liquid that dries clear, adds translucence to paint and is key to most decorative paint effects.

Key questions

DESIGN TIP

FIND A STARTING POINT
When choosing a color scheme, try to find a starting point to make the job easier. It can be your walls, floors, a favorite object or painting, or furniture that will be part of the finished room.

Before choosing the colors you'll use in a room, you'll need to answer the same questions an interior decorator would ask:

■ How permanent will this color be? If you plan to repaint in a few years, experiment with a bold palette; be more conservative if you are planning to sell the house.

■ What is your decorating style: eclectic, cottage, French country, or modern? The colors and color combinations associated with decorating styles can serve as starting points for your color scheme.

■ Which of the existing colors in the room will remain the same; which will change? Is the carpet staying, or will you change it as part of your new color scheme?

■ Which furnishings and window coverings will stay? Keep in mind when redecorating that it is far less expensive to change the color of a wall than to replace furnishings. Paint is your best decorating deal.

■ How much natural light enters the room during the day? Sunshine enters south windows much of the day. East or west windows receive direct sun only in morning or afternoon. North windows receive indirect sunlight. The type of light affects how you perceive the color (see pages 29–32).

■ What is the main source of light at night: fluorescent or incandescent? Like daylight, the type of artificial light affects how people see color.

■ At what times of day will the room be used most? Think about the lighting in a room during its peak activity, and select your colors accordingly.

■ What are the dominant colors in adjacent rooms? If another room is seen through a doorway, consider its color a part of the overall color scheme.

■ Would you like to make the room appear larger or smaller? Color can make a low ceiling appear higher or a high ceiling appear lower.

■ What mood are you trying to create? Is this a space for quiet reflection and reading, for unwinding after a hard day at the office, for pampering yourself and preparing to face the world, or for assembling intricate ship models?

The time and thought invested in answering these questions will be repaid many times in a home that reflects your personality and suits your needs.

You'll select color with more confidence when you answer some basic color and design questions.

Color has powerful effects on spaces and the people who live in them. That's why it is important that everyone who shares a space helps select its colors. Start by looking together at interior design books and magazines. Take note of pleasing colors and schemes. When you agree on a color scheme, match paint chips to the colors you like.

The color wheel

When you understand the relationships between colors, you'll be more confident combining them.

A color wheel organizes the visible spectrum of colors and shows the relationships between them. There are 12 pure colors on the most commonly used color wheel:

Three primary colors, red, yellow, and blue, are equally spaced around the color wheel. They are called primary because they cannot be derived by mixing other colors.

Three secondary colors, orange, green, and violet, are derived by mixing equal parts of the primary colors:

red + yellow = orange
yellow + blue = green
blue + red = violet

Six tertiary colors result from mixing equal parts of primary colors with their adjacent secondary colors:

red + orange = red-orange
red + violet = red-violet
yellow + orange = yellow-orange
yellow + green = yellow-green
blue + green = blue-green
blue + violet = blue-violet

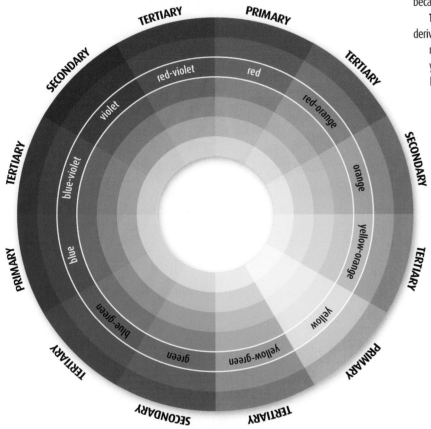

The color wheel defines the relationship between colors. Pure colors, those which have not been mixed with white or black, are on the third ring from the outside of the color wheel.

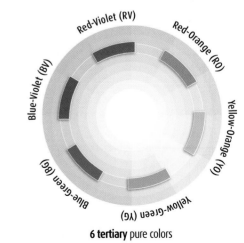

3 primary pure colors

3 secondary pure colors

6 tertiary pure colors

Help from Paint Companies

The color wheel helps you understand how colors relate to each other, but it can still be a challenge to choose the exact shades you want when you're standing in front of racks of paint cards. One of the ways paint companies have tried to make the job easier is to group colors into collections or palettes of hues that are guaranteed to work well together. The collection's name evokes a mood or style to help you identify the one that most appeals to you. A palette called "Modern Elegance," for example, suggests clean lines and contemporary furnishings, while "Country Comfort" evokes friendly, warm spaces with vintage fabrics and white-painted farmhouse chairs. A new line of paints exclusive to The Home Depot is called "Origenes." It's designed with Spanish-speaking consumers in mind and includes colors that reflect Latino cultural preferences. Within any of these paint collections, you'll find a full range of colors in coordinated tints and shades, so that whatever combination you decide on will produce a satisfying result. Look for color collections for both interiors and outdoor living spaces in the Color Solutions Center at The Home Depot.

Black and white

Colors outside and inside the ring of pure colors on the color wheel result from adding black or white.

Black is the absence of all light. Black paint absorbs all wavelengths of light, reflecting no light of any color. That is why the inside of a closet (no light) and a black object (no reflected light) are both perceived as black.

White is the presence of all colors. It is what the eye sees when struck by all colors of the spectrum, with natural sunlight serving as the standard source. White paint is white simply because it reflects all wavelengths of light equally.

Grays are mixtures of black and white. They are commonly specified as percentages of black.

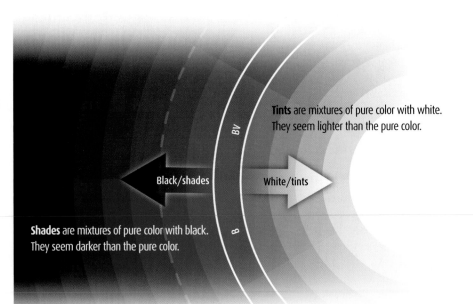

Tints are mixtures of pure color with white. They seem lighter than the pure color.

Black/shades

White/tints

Shades are mixtures of pure color with black. They seem darker than the pure color.

Hue, intensity, and value

The undiluted color from which a tint or shade is derived is referred to as its hue. The three primary, three secondary, and six tertiary pure colors of the color wheel (page 23) are all hues. So are the infinite number of colors that result from mixing these 12 pure hues.

Tints and shades are lighter and darker than the pure hue, but all share the same hue.

Colors are often described in professional circles by another set of terms: hue, intensity, and value.

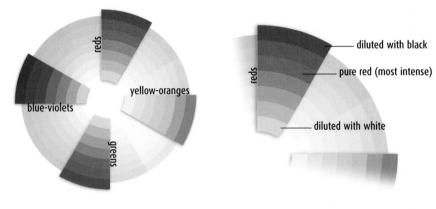

Tints and shades from the same slice of the color wheel are all the same hue.

A color is most intense in its pure form. Add white for a less intense tint; add black for a less intense shade.

Intensity (purity)

The purity of a color is referred to as its intensity. The most intense version of any color is the pure color, with no black or white added.

When white is added to a pure color, it diminishes the intensity by diluting the color. This is called tinting the color, and the lighter the tint, the closer it is to the center of the color wheel.

When black is added to a pure color, it produces darker, less intense derivatives of that color. This is called shading a color; the darker the shade, the closer it is toward the outside of the color wheel.

Select carefully. Many color designers prefer to stay within the same range of intensity when using different colors. In most cases, the pure color, with no black or white added, is used as an accent color.

Value (brightness)

The brightness of a color, as registered by a photographer's light meter or in a black–and–white photograph, is its value.

Adding white to a color increases its value. Adding black to a color decreases its value.

A monochromatic color scheme using tints and shades of a single hue thus contains a range of values.

Color values are particularly evident in black-and-white photos. High and low values create contrast and depth.

Basic color schemes

With the color wheel, you can design color palettes that are exciting or tranquil, bright or subdued.

One way to devise a color scheme is to choose a favorite color and then use the color wheel to select related or contrasting hues. The schemes on these pages show some examples of that approach. If you want to use pure, bright colors, remember that lower grades of paint use black to help hide imperfections, which diminishes the intensity of the pure color. To get pure colors, you'll have to use more expensive paint.

Monochromatic colors

The tints and shades of a single color are monochromatic, or one color. (For example, color cards usually show paint chips in a range of tints and shades for one color.) A color scheme using tints and shades of a single color is called a monochromatic color scheme.

Use a monochromatic color scheme to create an aura of serenity, elegance, and unity. Monochromatic colors do not compete; they cooperate. The infinite number of tints and shades can provide emphasis and variety or can be used to focus attention on a particular object or area of a room.

Monochromatic color schemes are perhaps the easiest to implement, but it's important to include a range of tints and shades or the results could be bland. The farther apart colors are on their slice of the color wheel, the more contrast there is between them. Select a medium tone or light tint for the walls and choose the darkest shade for the rug, sofa, or accessories. Use a mix of medium tones to tie the scheme together.

Start with white and add color. Monochromatic color schemes often work best starting from white. For example, begin with a white ceiling. Paint the walls in a slightly red tint (light pink). Paint the window and door casings and the baseboards a stronger tint of that same red. Create a tonal contrast for the doors and window sashes by adding gray to the color you used for the door and window casings.

This slice of the color wheel shows the tints and shades of blue that you could use to create a monochromatic color scheme.

Bathroom blues. Note the interesting variety of tints and shades—all variations of a single color. A white ceiling would reflect the blue of the walls and furnishings, evoking a sense of airiness.

Triadic colors

Three colors that are equidistant from each other around the color wheel are triadic colors. As you can see in the photo (right), a triadic color scheme of the primary colors can stimulate visual excitement. Triads of nonprimary colors are nearly as strong. They create interest through contrast.

Use tints and shades. To moderate the visual excitement of a triadic color scheme, use tints or shades instead of pure colors. For no-fail results, select colors from the same ring of the color wheel either inside or outside the third ring. For a more subtle effect, choose hues from different rings as in the bathroom (right).

The closer a color is to the center of the color wheel, the more restful it is on the eye. If a color combination is too dark, select lighter tints. If it is too light, substitute darker shades.

Bright yellow, medium blue, and rust red form a triadic scheme using hues from different rings on the wheel. Note that white and ivory accents can lighten a scheme without changing the color relationships.

The color wheel shows tints and shades of red, yellow, and blue.

Analogous colors

Colors that are side by side on the color wheel are analogous, or adjacent.

The contrast between analogous colors evokes a feeling of greater depth than monochromatic color schemes offer. To add more depth, use a variety of tints and shades.

Stimulate serenity. Use an analogous color scheme when you want to create a softer, less intense atmosphere while maintaining visual activity. Use pure colors to emphasize a major design element, to create visual movement, or to accent and ground a light, pastel scheme.

In an analogous color scheme, texture, pattern, and surrounding colors all work together to create a sense of harmony.

Based on blue and blue-violet, this color scheme uses texture as well as tints and shades to create a color palette with depth and contrast. Adding violet and blue green extends the color range and is still analogous.

The color wheel shows tints and shades of blue and blue-violet.

Complementary colors

Two colors positioned exactly opposite each other on the color wheel are said to be complementary. Color schemes that use tints and shades of colors opposite each other are complementary color schemes.

You might expect that pairing colors spaced the maximum distance apart on the color wheel would produce discordance. On the contrary, complementary schemes are commonly found in nature, such as the red and green combination of rose petal and leaf.

When you want to create a dynamic color scheme with snap and style, go with a complementary color scheme. Toning down the hues with gray can produce subdued color contrasts that are still quite visually stimulating.

The color wheel shows tints and shades of red and green.

The complementary colors of pink and soft green create a relaxed color scheme that evokes cottage-style comfort. Deeper reds and greens work well in formal rooms.

Analogous with complementary accents

Combining analogous colors with a complementary accent adds zing to a harmonious scheme. A closely related color scheme, the split complementary, pairs a color with those on each side of its complement.

Make a statement. Use either of these color schemes when you want to create a strong visual impact. To soften the contrast, try tints or shades instead of pure colors.

A vivid color is often best to use as an accent in three or four strategic locations. Or create a single focal point by using an accent color on one object or a major design element.

The color wheel shows tints and shades of orange, yellow-orange, and blue-violet.

Bold, bright colors make this shelf a focal point. Orange and yellow elements represent an analogous pairing, while the lavender complement in the artwork supplies a cool, balancing accent.

How light affects color

Color is a reflection of light. Thus the source and type of light play major roles in how the eye perceives color.

Natural daylight. Daylight is known as the perfect light source because the human eye has adapted to it over thousands of years. It is characterized by having nearly uniform intensity over the entire visible spectrum of colors.

The spectrum shown in the top photograph is that of the noon sun, when atmospheric absorption is at a minimum. Near sunrise and sunset the sun's rays have to traverse more of the atmosphere. The shorter wavelengths (blues and violets) are absorbed and scattered, shifting the spectrum toward the warmer reds.

Incandescent light. Incandescent lamps emit a greater percentage of long-wave radiation (reds) than the sun. As a result, objects they illuminate appear redder and warmer than under sunlight.

This effect is enhanced by dimmer controls. The dimmer reduces the power going to the lamp, lowering the temperature of the filament. As a result, the filament color shifts from yellow-white toward red.

Fluorescent light. Fluorescent lamps contain mercury atoms, which emit ultraviolet radiation when struck by electrons. This radiation is not visible, but it excites the phosphors coating the inside of the bulb, causing it to re-emit visible radiation in several peaks. One of the peaks is near the blue end of the visible spectrum. The light from the classic cool white bulb is distinctly bluer, or cooler, than sunlight.

Manufacturers have developed mixes of phosphors that closely match natural daylight. Several bulb types are designated "daylight" and "warm white."

NATURAL DAYLIGHT

INCANDESCENT LIGHT

The kind of light in which a color is viewed determines how it will be perceived.

FLUORESCENT LIGHT

Effects of the light sources

Consider the impact of light on color when you make your color selections.

Natural lighting. Illuminated solely by the daylight filtering through the window, the colors in the bathroom (right) appear natural.

When selecting colors for a room that has large windows and is used predominantly during daylight hours, view samples in your home in daylight.

Incandescent lamps. Illuminated by incandescent wall lamps, the same bathroom has a warmer appearance (below).

When selecting colors, take note of the time of day a room is most often used. When you're selecting colors for a room used primarily before sunrise and after sunset, choose them under the lighting used in the room.

Fluorescent lamps. Illuminated this time by a cool white overhead fluorescent fixture, the bathroom seems cold and otherworldly (bottom right).

Fluorescent light offers low-energy usage. Install lamps that more closely approximate daylight, or select warmer colors for the room. In either case, select the colors from color chips viewed under the type of lamp you plan to install.

NATURAL LIGHTING

INCANDESCENT LAMPS

FLUORESCENT LAMPS

Illumination level

The amount of light falling on surfaces alters our interpretation of their colors. Even though the difference in perception is one of value rather than hue, it is no less important than the effect of light sources described on page 30.

A lighter tint. Bright light falling on a surface increases the amount of light reflected back to our eye from the white component in a tint, but not from any black component. Thus, the value, or brightness, of the surface color increases in bright light. This makes objects appear more like a lighter tint.

A darker shade. Conversely, dimmer light falling on the surface decreases the white-reflected component. This decreases the intensity and value of a color, making it look like a darker shade of the same color.

When you select colors, do so with a careful eye toward the amount of light that is generally used in a room. For instance, if you want to brighten a room that has a low level of illumination, use lighter tints.

Bright lighting seems to lighten colors.

Dim lighting seems to darken colors.

Choose kitchen colors based on when the room is used most. A light, creamy yellow seen in morning light will feel bright and cheerful.

Choose dining room colors at night. Without natural light, the colors tend to appear darker than in daylight.

Reflected light source

Do you know why the sea appears blue under a blue sky, but gray under a gray sky? Seawater is colorless; you see the reflection of the light illuminating it—skylight.

White surfaces reflect all colors. Thus, a painted surface with a white component (tint) will reflect some of the color of the light reflected onto it.

Floors, ceilings, even carpets and furnishings can change your perceptions of the wall color.

White walls with light reflecting from white carpet.

White walls with light reflecting from red carpet.

Sheen/Finish (paint reflectivity)

Sheen or finish is a measure of the reflectivity of paint. The greater the sheen—increasing from flat through gloss—the higher the percentage of incident light reflected from the surface.

If the reflected light is white, as it would be from a white wall or ceiling, what the eye perceives is white light coming from the reflective surface.

That is why greater sheen has the same effect as greater illumination level: Sheen increases the value (brightness) of the surface.

Most paints are available in at least four of the five sheens: flat, eggshell, satin, semigloss, and gloss. Use gloss paint to brighten a room with little incident light; use flat or eggshell paint to reduce reflectivity.

The five paint sheens, from left to right: flat, eggshell, satin, semigloss, and gloss.

2

CHOOSING COLORS

Color matching

Paint departments of home centers and decorating centers typically offer thousands of color chips that you can use to develop your color scheme. Questions the customer always asks are: "How accurate are these colors? Is this really what the paint will look like on my walls?"

Color selection tips. Paint manufacturers strive to make the chips as accurate as possible. But, as with any tool, the proper use is up to you:

- All colors look different under different light sources (see pages 29–31). Compare several chips under the lighting conditions the room will ultimately have. Check the colors morning, noon, and night, because the lighting conditions probably will change.
- All colored paints darken as they dry. Before you conclude that the paint you just purchased doesn't match the chip, dry a swatch with a blow dryer. The staff may do this for you at the store.
- If you want a pastel or medium tone, go three shades lighter than the color you think you want, and you'll likely be satisfied with the result.

Test panels

To avoid costly mistakes, paint test panels or practice boards until you get the color you want. Buy quarts of the colors you're considering and apply them to 2×2-foot panels of primed drywall or foam-core panels, available at paint centers or art supply stores. For best results, prime the boards and apply two coats of paint as you would on the wall, allowing the paint to dry 24 hours between coats. Place the boards in various areas of the room and view them under all lighting conditions for at least a day and a night. Also consider how the test colors work with surrounding colors, furniture, and works of art, as well as light sources.

Paint darkens as it dries, so let the first coat dry thoroughly before you judge its success.

WORK SMARTER

STASH THE CHIPS
Tape the color chips under the coverplate of a light switch. If you need paint for a touch up, the formula will be at your fingertips.

A color chip rarely appears to be the same color as liquid paint in the can.

Paint a sample board and blow-dry it on the no-heat setting. The result will be closer to the color you selected.

Wet

Blow-dried

After one week

Liquid paint tends to look lighter than its final color. Even blow-drying the sample may not give you an accurate color match. You'll realize the final color only after the paint has cured.

Computer matching

What if you need to repaint only one wall of a room and you don't have any of the old paint? Or what if you want to match the trim paint to one of the colors in a room's wallpaper? In the past, a good painter could tint a paint on-site to match existing colors, but it required a good eye and years of experience. Today, computer technology takes much of the guesswork out of color matching.

The technology edge. If you provide a flat, opaque, solid sample of the color (the size of a quarter) that you want to match, the computer will analyze the sample and print a formula for mixing the paint.

Can you get a perfect match? If you expect the match to be close you will usually be satisfied. But if you're looking for an exact match you may be disappointed. The computer will also have difficulty matching colors from a piece of fabric or the pages of a magazine because the colors for printed material are created differently than they are for paint.

Note that some color chips are patented by the manufacturer, and it's illegal for the paint center to match the color. And using the formula for one brand to mix paint in another brand isn't recommended because it won't yield the true color.

With the computerized results, an almost exact color match can be formulated. Get two copies of the formula; tape one to the lid of the can, and keep the other in a safe place.

What color is this wall?

If you're tempted to choose a wall color based on a photo in a magazine or book, remember that the color you're seeing isn't a single, uniform hue but rather a range of tints and tones, depending on whether the color is in light or shadow. In the photo above, the wall color appears more yellowish near the lamps, more blue in the naturally lit areas and more gray in the shadows near the ceiling. In addition, the printing process translates the colors in film into tiny dots of magenta, cyan, yellow, and black. That's why computer matching isn't reliable with printed images—they are made up of dots rather than solid color. If you fall in love with a color in a photo, try to isolate which part of the photo you like best and look for paint chips that are similar in color. Then try test panels to see how the color or colors look in the lighting conditions in your home.

Using glazes

Glaze is a neutral paint formula to which no pigment has been added. For most decorative paint finishes it is mixed with paint to provide transparency and to slow the drying time, keeping the paint "open" or wet longer so you can rub, rag, stipple, or blend as needed to create the faux effect. The glaze is latex based, available in paint departments. Although it looks milky when first opened, it is semitransparent when dry.

Mixing glaze. Manufacturers usually recommend mixing one part paint with four parts glaze, so you would need 1 quart of paint for 1 gallon of glaze. You may find, however, that this mixture is too thin or too thick for the effect you want to achieve. To experiment, prime and paint a sample board with the base coat you're going to be using and let the paint dry. After the base color has dried, mix paint and glaze in varying proportions, and apply them to see how each looks over the base coat. For example, try three paint/glaze mixtures in small disposable cups: one part paint to eight parts glaze; one part paint to four parts glaze; and equal parts paint and glaze. When you find the ratio you like best, write it down, so you can duplicate it if the room requires more than one batch of glaze.

Glaze coverage. The amount of glaze used (coverage) depends on the application technique. When the effect is created by applying and then removing glaze, the expected coverage is roughly the same as that of a regular interior latex paint top coat: 400 square feet per gallon of glaze. When the effect is created by selectively adding a partial coat of glaze, the coverage may be doubled or more (you'll use half the glaze or less).

Mix enough glaze to finish one wall. It's better to have too much than too little. A bucket with printed measurements makes it easier to keep track of the proportion of glaze to paint so you can repeat the formula for each wall. One gallon of glaze and one quart of paint are usually enough to cover a 25×20-foot room.

WORK SMARTER

THE RIGHT SHEEN
For the most depth and translucency, professionals recommend using base coats with finishes that range form satin to semigloss. Flat paint doesn't have the oomph to give you the depth needed to bring painting effects to life.

CLOSER LOOK

MIXING CUSTOM GLAZES
Once you're familiar with faux techniques, you can try mixing you own glazes for special effects. The products can be purchased at paint centers. The basic formula is:

- 1 part acrylic latex paint.
- 1 part acrylic glazing medium.
- 1 part water.
- 2 ounces/gallon gel retarder.

To dilute the effect, or color intensity, of the glaze add more glazing medium. To thin the consistency for easier application, add water. To extend the drying time, add gel retarder.

Room painting basics

t's true that paint is the easiest and fastest way to give your rooms a facelift, but it's still an investment of time and money. That's why you want to be sure to do it right—and doing it right includes taking a little extra time up front to prepare surfaces properly. No matter how expensive the paint, it won't hide existing surface flaws. In this chapter you'll learn how to ensure that

your surface is smooth, clean, and ready for paint. You'll also learn how to choose the right primer. Remember that primer isn't simply diluted paint—it's like double-sided adhesive tape. It bonds to the existing surface and in turn "grabs" the paint and ensures good adhesion. For best results, choose a primer of the same brand as the paint you select. Tinting the primer can give you a headstart on getting good color coverage and is

Chapter 3 highlights

PROTECTING SURFACES
No matter how careful you are, paint can spatter or drip. You'll save time in the long run if you protect surfaces first.
 38

COMPLETE WALL PREP
Don't cut corners. To guarantee a good finish, repair small cracks and holes and remove stains and mildew before you paint.
 40

PRIMING IS ESSENTIAL
Priming helps you achieve a professional-looking paint job. Here's a guide to types of primers and which to use for your job.
 42

USING BRUSHES
Think you know how to use a paintbrush? Check out these tips to see how to get beautiful results.
 **44**

USING A PAINT ROLLER
Here's the low-down on using a paint roller to apply paint efficiently. Think "W."
 46

PAINTING CEILINGS
You may not paint the ceiling as often as you paint the walls, but these tips will help you do it right.
 47

PAINTING WALLS
It's time for the base coat. Once you complete this step, you're ready for the decorative techniques in Chapter 4.
 50

CLEANING SPILLS
Cleaning up spills and spatters is easier if you catch them as you go.
 53

Well-painted trim adds a simple finishing touch to the dramatic effect of the color wash on the walls. A good paint job is the result of taking the time to execute each step in the painting process carefully.

recommended if you're working with dark colors. The appropriate primer for dark colors may depend on your region: In the South, where the light is strong, experts recommend a gray primer for red paint; in the Midwest, where the light is softer, a pink primer gives more brilliant results. Always calculate paint quantities carefully, since custom-mixed paints can't be returned. Darker colors will need three to four coats, even with a primer.

Protecting surfaces

Good prep means a faster, neater, and more successful job. Protecting surrounding surfaces is essential.

Paint always ends up where you don't want it. You can stop and clean as you go, or you can protect vulnerable surfaces before you start, saving you time in the long run. Remove the furniture, if possible, and protect floors, windows, doors, trim and baseboards, and light fixtures. Protect yourself with an old long-sleeved shirt and pants—or purchase painter's coveralls and hoods.

Spatter-proof the room. To protect large surfaces and furnishings, invest in a good drop cloth. You will generally find three types:

- Polyethylene sheeting (poly) is inexpensive but slippery (see "Buyer's Guide" below).
- Canvas is the toughest and most expensive, but water-based (latex) paints can leak through it.
- Paper/poly (fuzzy paper on one side and plastic on the other) is waterproof, less slippery than poly, and less expensive than canvas.

To protect trim and other margins, use blue painter's tape—it's more expensive than ordinary masking tape but its lower-tack adhesive won't damage finished surfaces when you remove it.

BUYER'S GUIDE

SELECT THE DROP CLOTH THAT'S RIGHT FOR EACH PAINT JOB Poly sheeting, the least expensive, is waterproof but slippery underfoot.

Canvas will last longest but is not waterproof; water-based (latex) paints probably will soak through it.

Paper/poly is a good compromise. It is waterproof and less slippery than poly sheeting.

A **painter's cap** keeps the spatters out of your hair when you're painting overhead.

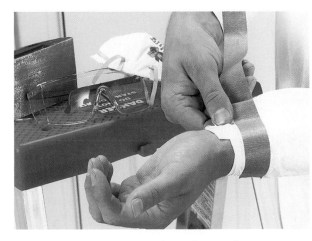

When sanding or spray-painting, cinch your sleeves and cuffs with masking tape.

A **painter's coverall** offers neck-to-toe protection and "breathes" to keep you cool.

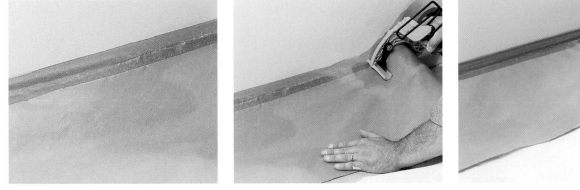

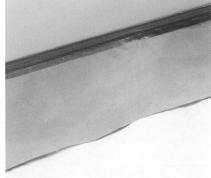

Blue painter's tape can remain for up to two weeks while prepping but must be removed immediately after painting.

Paper masking combined with self-adhesive blue painter's tape protects baseboards and trim. Burnish the edge to prevent paint leaking under it.

Slip a paper/poly drop cloth under the baseboard masking for complete floor protection.

Complete wall prep

✓ STUFF YOU'LL NEED

TOOLS: Bucket, rubber gloves, drop cloth, 4-foot stepladder, sponge, phillips screwdriver, 3-inch putty knife, sanding block, 2-inch nylon brush

MATERIALS: 12-inch baseboard masking, blue painter's tape, bleach, water, lightweight crack filler, 220-grit sandpaper, tack cloth, oil-based or latex stain-blocking primer, TSP substitute

🔍 CLOSER LOOK

SQUEAKY-CLEAN WALLS
Trisodium phosphate (TSP), a nonsudsing soap that is 100 percent phosphate, is the most powerful cleaner you can buy. But phosphate also causes algae blooms in water bodies, so its use has been restricted in some areas. Also, TSP will prevent paint from bonding, so you must rinse the surface several times with fresh water to remove all residue. Check the label for usage instructions.

🖌 TOOL SAVVY

WET-SANDING
One of the most annoying parts of sanding plaster and joint compound is the flourlike dust that is produced. To minimize the dust, use a drywall wet-sander: a sponge with coarse abrasive on one side and fine abrasive on the other side. Use the coarse side to level ridges and high spots; use the fine side to smooth.

No amount of paint, no matter how high its quality, will cover flaws in the wall beneath or adhere well to dirty walls. Thus, proper preparation, whether for a single coat of paint or decorative paint finish, is the most important step of any painting project.

Don't cut corners—if you don't do it right the first time, you'll do it over again.

Before painting, mark any marred wall areas with a soft-lead pencil so you don't overlook needed repairs.

1 COVER AREA WITH DROP CLOTHS
Move furniture away from walls and protect floor and baseboards with 12-inch baseboard masking and a paper/poly drop cloth.

2 REPAIR SMALL CRACKS AND HOLES
Set popped nails or screws, repair cracks and holes, and fill dents with lightweight crack filler.

3 REMOVE STAINS AND MILDEW
Treat any areas of mildew with a 3-to-1 water/bleach solution (see page 41). If you are sensitive to bleach, protect your hands and eyes.

4 SAND WITH A SANDING BLOCK
Let the crack filler dry according to the manufacturer's instructions, then sand the wall using a sanding block with 220-grit sandpaper.

5
CLEAN THE WALLS
Clean with a TSP solution if the surfaces are greasy (see "Closer Look" opposite). Otherwise, use a TSP substitute, which does not need rinsing. Let the wall dry overnight.

6
SPOT-PRIME REPAIRED AREAS
Spot-prime all of the repaired areas with a latex stain-blocking primer. If stains are still bleeding through, use an oil-based primer.

Treat stains and mildew

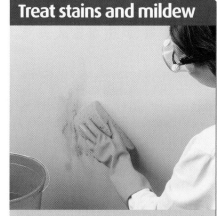

Before you prime or paint, remove stains and mildew. It takes elbow grease, but cleaning will save time in the long run because you won't have to repaint. To treat, mix three parts water to one part bleach in a plastic bucket. Apply liberally with a sponge. Apply again after 20 minutes. Rinse thoroughly with clean, fresh water.

Don't mix bleach with other household cleaners. Household cleaners most often contain ammonia, which will react with the bleach to produce toxic fumes.

Inhaling such fumes can cause dizziness, nausea, cramps, or extreme illness. If you do breathe such fumes, get outside and breathe fresh air until your symptoms disappear.

Removing gloss

It's almost impossible for paint to adhere to a glossy surface, because a glossy surface lacks what painters call "tooth," or roughness, which gives the paint something to stick to. To detect gloss, use a bright light with a reflector to shield your eyes.

It doesn't take much to create tooth—a light sanding or use of a chemical deglosser will do the trick. When the surface ceases to be reflective, it's ready to paint.

OLD vs. NEW

LIQUID DEGLOSSER
If the paint is sound and smooth enough that it doesn't require sanding, prepping with a liquid deglosser is a lot simpler. Be sure to follow the manufacturer's directions.

Wear neoprene rubber gloves, goggles, and a respirator recommended by the deglosser manufacturer.

1
SAND LIGHTLY UNTIL SMOOTH
Fill gaps in trim and baseboard with paintable caulk, then sand lightly with 220-grit sandpaper. Use a sanding block for flat surfaces, a brass-wire brush for fluted surfaces.

2
REMOVE DUST WITH A TACK CLOTH
Remove the sanding or brushing residue with a tack cloth so the surface is smooth and clean.

Priming is essential

STUFF YOU'LL NEED

TOOLS: Drop cloth, paint tray, paint can opener or screwdriver, stir stick, 2-inch brush, 9-inch roller with appropriate nap, roller extension handle, 4-foot stepladder, drywall sanding block

MATERIALS: Appropriate primer, 12-inch baseboard masking, blue painter's tape, 220-grit sandpaper

WORK SMARTER

DARK COLORS

You might think that darker colors hide better, but it's not true. When painting a dark, rich color, you must use a tinted primer and at least three coats of paint to get a smooth, even finish.

Priming helps ensure a professional-looking paint job. It isn't just a way to sell you one more paint product, and it isn't just watered-down paint. Primer is a specially formulated product designed to:

- Increase adhesion
- Help the finish coat develop maximum sheen
- Give the finish coat a uniform appearance
- Increase the finish coat coverage
- Block stains from water, dirt, smoke, etc.
- Block tannins from aromatic woods
- Block resins from knots and pitch pockets
- Add to corrosion resistance over metals

Primed for success

Priming involves the same steps as painting the finish coat on the wall.

To prepare all surfaces for priming, first repair and clean them. Cover all surfaces you do not plan to paint; primer can be as difficult to remove as paint. And it spatters just as much! Primers have different windows of time that they retain tooth for good adhesion, from 24 hours to 30 days. Check the label on the can to determine whether you need to apply the finish paint within a day or two of priming.

Priming the wall is the final step before you actually paint it.

1 TINT PRIMER FOR BEST RESULTS
Most primers can be tinted, and tinting will ensure good coverage for the finish coat. But too much tint will dilute the primer and reduce its efficiency. Usually a primer can be tinted by no more than 25 percent of the formula for the color you've chosen; follow the recommendations of the manufacturer.

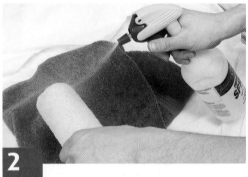

2 SPRAY ROLLER OR BRUSH
Dampen your roller or brush to get off to a fast start. Use water for latex, paint thinner for alkyd.

Priming different surfaces

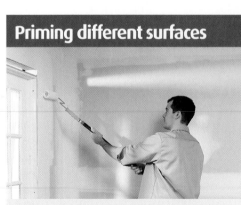

Prime new drywall to conceal the difference between taped and untaped areas.

Prime new wood, old bare wood, and pressure-treated lumber with a stain-killing primer to block resins and tannins in the wood and create a smooth and seamless finished surface. Let the primer dry thoroughly, according to the manufacturer's instructions, before applying the finish color.

3

CUT IN CORNERS

Pick your starting point and cut in the corner with a 2-inch sash brush or a corner pad. Cut in the first 3 to 4 feet along the ceiling too.

4

ROLL ON PRIMER

Apply the primer using a 9-inch roller with the appropriate nap. Start with a single vertical strip at the cut-in corner.

5

PAINT A W PATTERN

Roll the remaining wall in 3×3-foot sections, working from top to bottom. Lay the primer down in a W, then fill in the gaps without lifting the roller.

Types of primer

Just as primer is different from finish paint, there are different primers for different problems and applications. **Apply all primers with adequate ventilation.**

1 **Polyvinyl acetate (PVA) latex primer** seals new drywall for painting. Both the paper face and joint compound are absorbent and would otherwise steal too much water from finish latex paint. It is not intended for trim or previously painted surfaces. Clean up with water.

2 **All-purpose primer** is a general term for any primer designed for maximum adhesion to impervious surfaces, such as metal, glass, tile, and thermoplastics, such as laminated plastic and melamine. It is harder to work with than a conventional latex primer, but the results are well worth the effort. Clean up with soap and water.

3 **Latex stain-blocking primer** is effective in stopping most staining materials from coming through the paint. For difficult stains, such as washable markers, use oil-based or alcohol-based primer instead. Clean up with warm, soapy water.

4 **Oil-based stain-blocking primer** effectively blocks crayon, permanent-marker, grease, and water stains. Even though it is a bit harder to work with, it's one of the rare ways to prevent an unremovable stain from bleeding through paint. Clean up with paint thinner.

5 **Alcohol-based, white-pigmented shellac** is impervious, exhibits excellent adhesion, and effectively blocks smoke stains and all of the tannins and resins in wood. It also inhibits pet odors. It is brittle and damaged by UV rays, however, so it is recommended only for interior use. Note that it is flammable and must be used with adequate ventilation. Clean up with denatured alcohol.

6 **Enamel undercoat** contains a higher percentage of solids and is used when maximum effect is desired in satin, semigloss, or gloss. Being hard, it can be sanded to produce the smoothest possible base for the finish coat. Clean up with soap and water.

CLOSER LOOK

WHY USE BOTH PAINT AND PRIMER?
Paint and primer perform two distinct and important functions, and to get a good job you can't use one without the other. Primer provides bonding and blocking. Paint provides durability and color.

GOOD IDEA

THE TAPE TEST
If the wall has been previously painted with latex, if there has been no patching, and if the paint is clean and adhering well, you may be able to consider the old paint to be the primer for the new.

Here is a test: Press a piece of transparent tape onto the old paint, then remove it. If the old paint comes off with the tape, you need to prime.

Using brushes

3

ROOM PAINTING BASICS

CLOSER LOOK

BRISTLE WISE
Don't press the bristles firmly against the side of the can or bucket. Pressure will collapse and empty the reservoir between the wood spacers, as seen in this cross-sectioned brush.

Quick tip

Don't hold the brush too tightly. Too much gripping pressure will tire your hand quickly and make painting a chore.

Learn to use a paintbrush properly by practicing these basic techniques and using the right brush for the job. Prime (wet) the brush with the right thinner (water for latex paint, mineral spirits for alkyd) before you dip it into paint. Brush out excess thinner and load the brush with paint.

One step at a time. Painting is a three-step process: Apply a brush load, spread the paint, then smooth it to an even finish. Start the second brush load at the wet edge of the first stroke, and paint toward the dry. Then paint back toward the wet area. Feather the two areas together with light strokes. Apply a heavy coat; it will flow and hide better than if you brush the paint out too thin.

Achieve stunning results by knowing how to properly use a high-quality paintbrush.

Hold the brush handle between your thumb and forefinger, with your other fingers on the ferrule.

Use your wrist and your arm when you paint. You'll have better control, and it's less tiring than using just your arm.

Dip the bristles only one-third of their length into the paint. This will keep paint from building up in the ferrule.

Tap both sides of the loaded brush on the side of the bucket. Dragging or pressing removes too much paint.

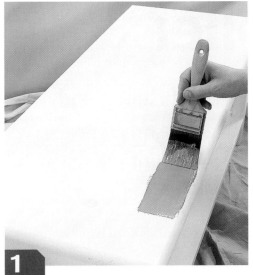

1
BRUSH AWAY FROM THE END
Start your first brush stroke one brush width from the end; brush away from the end.

2
BRUSH TOWARD THE END
Return to the starting point and brush toward the end. Spread, then smooth with a light touch.

3
START AGAIN AT THE WET EDGE
To avoid overlap marks, start subsequent strokes at the wet edge of the previous stroke and paint toward dry.

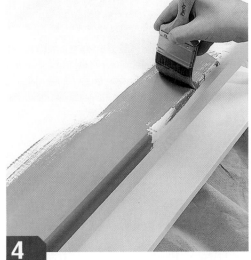

4
FEATHER AND BLEND AREAS TOGETHER
Paint back toward the wet area. Feather the two areas together with light strokes.

WORK SMARTER

DON'T OVERBRUSH
Overbrushing results in what the pros call "roping," which are the lines the brush leaves in the paint because it was already partially dried when it was painted over. The general rule is, "Let it dry and fix it later."

REAL WORLD

DRIED ISN'T CURED
There's a big difference between paint that is dry to the touch and paint that has cured, meaning that all the liquid has evaporated and the color has reached maturity. A paint can be dry to the touch in several hours, but it can take as long as 30 days to fully mature and cure. Humidity and temperature also affect curing time. Check the label for the manufacturer's guidelines.

Using a paint roller

When the can says it covers 400 square feet, it isn't kidding; most pros don't expect to get more than 300 to 350 feet. Stretching paint for extended coverage is the most common mistake beginning painters make. You'll know you've got the right amount of paint for good coverage on your roller when it doesn't slide or skip, rolls on smoothly, and doesn't drip. Let the roller do the work; use only enough pressure to get the paint on the wall.

For speed, efficiency, and even coverage on a large space, use a paint roller.

1

LIGHTLY DAMPEN THE ROLLER

Prime the roller cover with a misting bottle filled with water (latex) or a rag doused in mineral spirits (alkyd) before starting. Remove excess liquid, or the first application will run.

2

DIP THE ROLLER INTO PAINT

Dip the roller cover into the tray and saturate it with paint. Then remove excess paint by gently rolling it back and forth on the grated part of the paint tray.

3

PAINT A W PATTERN

Start at a corner and roll on an 18×18-inch W pattern. If the paint drips, start with an upstroke, making an M.

TIMESAVER

POWER UP

For a big job, a power roller speeds painting and reduces cleanup. Paint is fed to the roller via a tube attached to a pump immersed in the paint can. Press the handle trigger to reload the roller with fresh paint.

4

FILL IN WITH PAINT

Fill in the W without lifting the roller. Continue down and across, blending sections together. Keep the roller wet with paint.

5

BACK-ROLL TO SMOOTH FINISH

After you finish a 3-foot-wide section, reload the roller lightly and back-roll from floor to ceiling. This smooths out the finish and removes lap marks, drips, and bare spots. Do not back-roll if the paint has already begun to dry or you'll simply pull the paint off the wall.

Painting ceilings

TOOLS: Screwdriver, drop cloth, paint tray, paint pad, 9-inch roller cover with the appropriate nap, roller cage with extension handle, paint tray, 4-foot stepladder, safety goggles, painter's cap

MATERIALS: Plastic bag(s), 2-inch blue painter's tape, primer, latex ceiling paint, clean cotton rag

WORK SMARTER

EXTENSION POLES

Extension poles make painting ceilings easier and more efficient. Poles that extend from 4 to 6 feet will allow you to roll the majority of the ceiling without having to use a ladder. The pole should be long enough that you can hold the bottom at hip level and the top at head level. Extension poles make rolling walls easier as well.

WORK SMARTER

A GOOD INVESTMENT

Much of the mess when painting a ceiling is from the drips that come when you're reaching from bucket to ceiling. A power roller eliminates the extra motion as well as most drips—and speeds things up!

Painting a ceiling? Invest in an extension pole, safety goggles, and a painter's cap. And use ceiling—not wall—paint. It comes in a variety of colors, all specially formulated to:

- Diffuse light from lamps, windows, and other sources of illumination
- Have a flat sheen, so the ceiling will have an even appearance
- Offer better spatter resistance for overhead rolling

Prep the ceiling before painting. Dust and grime accumulate, making it virtually impossible for paint to adhere. Mildew and water stains will bleed through even the best of paint. Cracks, mars, and dents are more visible in the artificial light that generally reflects off ceilings.

Keys to superior ceiling results are careful, thorough preparation, priming, and the use of quality paint.

Add color. The ceiling can be an important part of your color palette. For instance, if you want to bring the ceiling "down" for a cozier room, paint it a darker color. For a light, airy feeling, paint the ceiling a very pale blue.

Ceilings are as easy to paint as the walls. Just do the necessary prep work and use the right tools.

SHUT OFF OVERHEAD LIGHT FIXTURES
Remove furniture from the room. Shut off overhead fixtures at the breaker or fuse box.

REMOVE OR COVER FIXTURES
Remove or bag the ceiling fixtures. Removal of the ceiling fixtures will make for a neater job, but you can also drop the cover plates and wrap the fixtures in plastic bags.

3 **MASK OFF THE WALL**

Mask off the tops of the walls with 2-inch blue painter's tape. One-inch tape would allow the roller to strike the wall.

4 **PROTECT AREA WITH DROP CLOTHS**

Cover the floor by overlapping drop cloths by at least 12 inches. Protect windows, doors, and trim, if necessary.

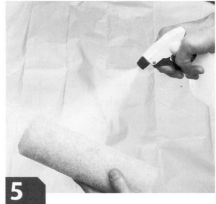

5 **DAMPEN THE ROLLER**

Prime the roller cover by spraying it with a misting bottle until it is just damp. Remove excess water before you begin painting.

6 **CUT IN THE CORNER**

To start, cut in one corner of the ceiling with a paint pad. Cut in only as much as you can roll out before the paint dries.

7 **ROLL ALONG THE WET EDGE TO BLEND AREAS**

Begin rolling over the still-wet cut-in strip. Keeping a wet edge prevents overlap marks in the finished ceiling. Load the roller regularly and roll slowly. Back-roll to blend the paint.

8 **WORK IN MANAGEABLE SECTIONS**

Work in sections to keep wet edges. Cut in with a pad or brush, apply paint with a roller, then roll out applied paint to blend the two areas.

GOOD IDEA

BETTER RESULTS
Roll in the direction of the shorter room dimension to minimize the drying time between passes. This gives you time to feather the wet paint, avoiding overlap marks.

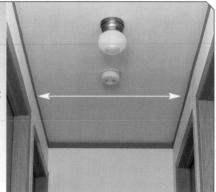

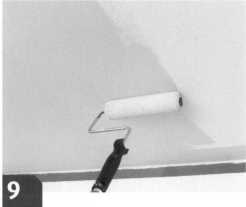

9 **VARY THE DIRECTION OF THE ROLLER**
Slightly vary the direction of your rolling. Perfectly straight rolling is more likely to show overlap marks.

10 **CONTINUE UNTIL THE SECTION IS DONE**
Continue applying paint, rolling out, and blending until the first cut-in section is finished.

11 **START ON THE NEXT SECTION**
Begin the next section by cutting in the wall/ceiling joint.

12 **REPEAT THE PROCESS**
Apply paint, roll out, and blend with the cut-in edge and the previous section.

13 **WIPE UP DRIPS AND SPATTERS**
Watch for drips and spatters. Wipe up immediately with a damp rag.

Painting popcorn ceilings

Popcorn ceilings have a water-soluble base, so water-based paints can cause the popcorn texture to come down as you roll on the paint. Before painting, seal the ceiling with a white-pigmented shellac.

Always paint with flat paint. Work the paint on in 2-foot squares with light pressure, crosshatch in one direction only, and don't re-roll. Once a section is finished, move on.

Painting walls

✓ STUFF YOU'LL NEED

TOOLS: Screwdriver, drop cloth, paint tray, 2-inch trim nylon or polyester brush, 9-inch roller cover with ⅜-inch nap, roller cage with extension handle, paint tray, 4-foot stepladder
MATERIALS: Paint test panels or sheet of drywall, blue painter's tape, masking tape, 12-inch baseboard masking, 5-gallon bucket, latex wall paint, clean cotton rag

📖 WORK SMARTER

ESTIMATING SQUARE FOOTAGE
The pros recommend covering no more than 300 to 400 square feet per gallon for good results. See page 12 of this book for a helpful guide to calculating how much paint you'll need for your room.

Changing the color scheme in a room is the fastest and least expensive decorating touch on the market.
　A quality wall paint is formulated to:
- Provide maximum covering.
- Have good scrub and burnish resistance.
- Resist stains from spills, ink markers, and crayons.

　If you are radically changing the colors or are applying a much darker color, a second coat is essential, and a third may be necessary to completely cover a wall.
　Start painting from a corner of the room that isn't hit by direct sunlight. Sunlit walls may be too hot for the paint to make its initial bond, possibly affecting the final cure. If the wall is warm to the touch, wait until it cools down before you apply the paint.

The basics of painting are easy to learn, and putting them into practice will make every painting job easier and faster!

1
PAINT TEST PANELS TO FIND THE RIGHT COLOR
Before finalizing your wall color choice, paint test panels with the colors you are considering. Purchase blank test panels from a paint center or make them from cut-up drywall, hardboard, or foamcore board. Compare candidate colors under all the lighting conditions you will find in the room over the course of a full day and evening.

2
REMOVE THE COVER PLATES
Remove all of the electrical cover plates on the wall. Reinstall the screws in the outlet box to avoid misplacing them.

3
COVER RECEPTACLES WITH PAINTER'S TAPE
Pull off dimmer knobs. Cover the switches and receptacles with masking tape.

4 **REMOVE OR COVER FURNITURE**

Remove all of the furniture or group it in the center of the room. Protect it from spatters with plastic or a drop cloth.

5 **PROTECT SURFACES FROM PAINT**

Mask any surfaces not to be painted, such as door and window casings, with blue painter's tape.

6 **PROTECT THE BASEBOARDS**

Mask off the baseboards with 12-inch baseboard masking, overlapping the floor drop cloth. (Clean the baseboards before taping to ensure good adhesion.)

7 **MIX ENOUGH PAINT TO COMPLETE THE ENTIRE JOB**

Box the paint (mix the contents of all the containers for consistency) in a 5-gallon bucket and stir.

8 **DAMPEN THE ROLLER AND PAINTBRUSH**

Prime the roller cover and cutting-in brush by wetting with a misting bottle (for latex paint). Remove excess water before applying paint.

9 **CUT IN AT THE CORNER**

Start by cutting in a corner with the brush. Cut in only as far as your arm will reach to make sure you keep a wet edge when you roll on the paint.

10 **ROLL OUT FROM THE WET EDGE**
Begin rolling by applying a vertical strip that overlaps the cut-in strip.

11 **PAINT A W PATTERN**
Roll paint in a W pattern, then spread the paint to fill in the pattern. Work in small sections so the paint doesn't begin to dry before you can fill in the section.

12 **BACK-ROLL TO BLEND THE SECTION**
Fill the roller with a light load and roll the wet paint from floor to ceiling to blend and finish each section. Let the first coat dry at least 12 hours before applying the second coat.

13 **MASK OFF WALL TO PAINT TRIM**
Give the wall paint a minimum of 24 hours to cure, then mask with blue painter's tape. If the wall isn't fully cured, mask with white quick-release tape so you won't remove paint when you remove the tape.

14 **PAINT THE TRIM IF DESIRED**
Don't puddle paint against the tape, however, or you'll pull off paint along with the tape when you remove it. Remove the tape immediately by pulling it down and away from the wall.

☀ **GOOD IDEA**

STOP SMART
Always finish a painting session at a natural divide (an inside or outside corner or a doorway). The differences in lighting prevent your eye from detecting subtle changes in color or sheen that may occur when you continue painting later.

Cleaning spills

S pills and spatters are inevitable when you paint. Even professionals dribble and drip occasionally. But the difference between the pros and most of the rest of us is that they clean up as they go.

On a nonporous surface, any spill needs to be wiped up immediately with a clean cloth while the paint is still liquid. If you're using latex paint, spray the splatter with clean water. Then wipe up the spill before you reload the brush.

Remove paint from fabric while it's still wet. The key is to dilute the paint with water, then wash it in a TSP solution.

You may not notice the paint on fabric until it has hardened. With latex paint, rub the fabric with an all-purpose cleaner (check the paint aisle for appropriate cleaners). With oil-based paint, try soap and water or use a brush cleaner. In both cases, wash as recommended on the cleaner label.

Dried paint can be tough to remove. You'll save time if you make a habit of cleaning up as you go.

BUYER'S GUIDE

COMMERCIAL SPOT REMOVERS
There are several brands of commercial spot removers especially formulated to remove latex paint that has dried on floors, baseboards, and trim. They do the job, but you're still better off dealing with drips and spatters before they dry completely. Follow the directions and provide adequate ventilation while you're using the product.

ROOM PAINTING BASICS

3

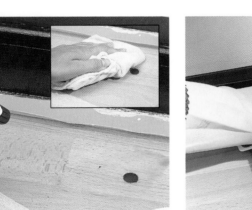

Keep a spray bottle of water handy when painting with latex. Spray drips and spatters and wipe immediately with a clean, soft cloth.

If the paint spots have hardened too much to wet and wipe, scrub them with a wet plastic scrub pad, then wipe up.

If a scrub pad doesn't work, pry the spots off carefully with a plastic or metal putty knife.

For oil-based spills, try wiping up drips with a dry cotton rag. If necessary, dampen the rag with a small amount of paint thinner or denatured alcohol.

Decorative techniques

Decorative finishes add dimension and personality to any room. In this chapter you'll find how-to instructions for 40 decorative painting techniques, along with complete tools lists and tips for success. Many techniques require that you mix paint with glaze medium to to create the look of fabric or stone or to give the illusion of dimension to your walls. Glaze adds transparency to paint, allowing the color underneath to show through. It also slows the drying time so that you can manipulate the colored glaze to achieve the desired effect. And if you don't like the results, you can wipe the glaze off and start over. For each technique you'll find the color names of the paints used in the photo; to find the brand names and paint numbers, turn to Resources and check the page-by-page listing. The "Time to Complete" figures include wall preparation, base-coating, and time to execute the technique, including drying times between steps.

Chapter 4 highlights

Suede

✓ STUFF YOU'LL NEED

SUEDE FINISH: Arrow Wood Marante
TOOLS: Drop cloth, paint tray, 2-inch tapered trim brush, 9-inch specialty finish roller, 3-inch latex paintbrush
MATERIALS: 2-inch low-tack painter's tape, stir sticks

🕐 TIME TO COMPLETE

Based on a 12×12 foot room,
8 foot ceiling
EXPERIENCED: 12 hrs.
HANDY: 14 hrs.
NOVICE: 16 hrs.

🐦 BEFORE YOU BEGIN

Prepare the surface according to pages 40–43. Prime the walls with a deep-tinted primer. Mask the ceiling, baseboards, and trim with low-tack painter's tape.

Arrow Wood Marante

This technique mimics the soft, touchable texture of suede. Created with a specialty finish roller and specially formulated paints, it's an easy technique to do, but it does require patience. Because the paint leaves a slightly rough coating that is not scrubbable, this technique is recommended for low-traffic areas such as dining rooms and bedrooms. The suede finish works best when applied over a smooth, dull surface. On the wall above, a dark brown paint was used for the base coat and the same dark brown was used for the top coat. For greater contrast (and therefore more dimension), use one color for the base coat and two values of the same color (one lighter and one darker) for the top coat. Note that the first coat will appear uneven and splotchy; the second coat wil even out the coverage. Avoid touching up areas that have already dried, because the touch-up will be noticeable. If you must take a break before you finish the room, try to stop at a corner so the stopping point won't be noticeable.

1 ROLL VERTICALLY FROM TOP TO BOTTOM

Using the tapered trim brush and the Arrow Wood Marante suede paint, trim the corners and ceiling lines in a section approximately 28 inches wide, or three roller cover widths. Roll the 9-inch specialty finish roller vertically from top to bottom, filling in the trimmed area. Continue the process of trimming and rolling on wet paint vertically with the 9-inch roller until the entire wall is finished. **This coat of paint will appear uneven.** Allow to dry.

2 BRUSH IN A CROSSHATCHING MOTION

Dip the 3-inch latex paintbrush into the Arrow Wood Marante suede paint. Brush the wall using random X strokes after each dip. Use sweeping, overlapping strokes. Continue crosshatching, moving quickly across the wall without overlapping into areas that have already started to dry. Drag the brush in an X pattern in the corners to avoid straight lines.

The finished wall will have softly modulated differences in tone, giving the wall the subtle dimension of brushed suede.

WORK SMARTER

UNEVEN EDGES
Start at the top of the wall and always move down, working in irregular shapes to avoid leaving any straight or square lines in the suede top coat.

Linen

✓ STUFF YOU'LL NEED

BASE COAT: Stucco White semigloss finish latex paint
GLAZE COAT: Alfalfa tinted glaze
TOOLS: Drop cloth, paint trays, standard roller frame with ¼-inch nap paint roller cover, 2-inch tapered trim brush, level with printed ruler, light green colored pencil, 7-inch linen weaver brush
MATERIALS: 2-inch low-tack painter's tape, stir sticks, lint-free cotton cloths

🕐 TIME TO COMPLETE

Based on a 12×12 foot room, 8 foot ceiling
EXPERIENCED: 9 hrs.
HANDY: 10 hrs.
NOVICE: 11 hrs.

🖐 BEFORE YOU BEGIN

Prepare the surface according to pages 40–43. Mask ceiling, baseboards, and trim with low-tack painter's tape. Base-coat the wall with Stucco White, using two coats if necessary. Leave the tape on and allow to dry overnight.

A dd a touch of elegance to plain walls with the woven look of linen. For this effect, a dry linen weaver brush is dragged horizontally, then vertically through wet glaze, exposing the base coat color. Use a light touch on the brush for a more delicate effect. This technique is not difficult, but it's even easier if you have a partner to apply the texture as soon as you roll on the glaze.

The linen effect works well in a casual living space with natural woodwork, such as a sunroom or living room. For a more sophisticated look, try a darker tone over a lighter tone. The specialty glaze used here contains tiny beads that leave a slight texture on the wall; the glaze has a satin finish, so it's more durable than the suede finish, but like suede, it's not scrubbable.

Stucco White

Alfalfa

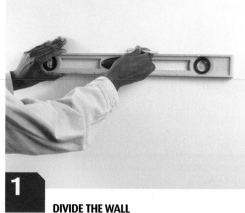

1

DIVIDE THE WALL
Using a level with printed measurements, divide the wall into vertical sections approximately 24 to 36 inches wide.

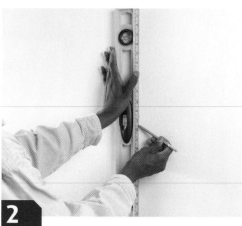

2

DRAW VERTICAL LINES
Extend the lines vertically using a light green colored pencil.

3 MASK OFF SECTIONS

Define the outside edges of alternating sections with low-tack painter's tape. To end a section in a corner, tape the edge of the adjoining wall where they meet in the corner. Press the edges of the tape firmly to prevent paint seeping underneath.

4 ROLL ON GLAZE

Using a paint roller with a ¼-inch nap roller cover, apply a thin layer of Alfalfa glaze over the taped-off section. Smooth out the roller marks with light, vertical strokes.

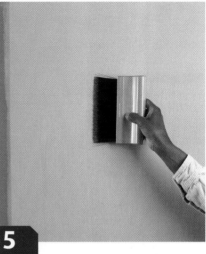

5 DRAG BRUSH HORIZONTALLY

Beginning at the top left-hand corner of the section, drag the dry linen weaver brush horizontally across the section, using smooth strokes. Each stroke should start and stop on the painter's tape. To reduce smudging, drag away from corners rather than into them. Continue dragging until the section is completed. Maintain even pressure on the brush as you drag it across.

6 KEEP THE BRUSH CLEAN

After each stroke, remove excess glaze from the brush with a lint-free cotton cloth.

7 DRAG BRUSH VERTICALLY

Working from top to bottom, drag the brush vertically down the section, using a light touch on the brush. Continue until the section is completed. Remove the strips of painter's tape immediately after completing the dragging. Let the glazed sections dry at least 24 hours, then tape off the remaining sections, placing the tape on top of the dried glaze along the edge where the two sections meet. Repeat Steps 4–7.

The linen effect is very subtle and sophisticated, an excellent choice for both formal and informal rooms.

Strié

✓ STUFF YOU'LL NEED

BASE COAT: Corn Husk Green satin finish latex paint

GLAZE COAT: Smokey Slate satin finish latex paint

TOOLS: Drop cloth, paint tray, standard roller frame with 9-inch roller cover, 2-inch tapered trim brush, level with printed ruler, light green or gray colored pencil, plastic container with printed measurements, 4-inch long bristle brush

MATERIALS: 2-inch low-tack painter's tape, stir sticks, glaze medium, lint-free cotton cloths

🕐 TIME TO COMPLETE

Based on a 12×12 foot room, 8 foot ceiling

EXPERIENCED: 6 hrs.

HANDY: 8 hrs.

NOVICE: 10 hrs.

🖐 BEFORE YOU BEGIN

Prepare the surface according to pages 40–43. Mask the ceiling, baseboards, and trim with low-tack painter's tape. Paint the entire wall in the Corn Husk Green base-coat color. Paint two coats if necessary. Leave tape on and allow to dry overnight.

Corn Husk Green

Smokey Slate

S trié is a subtly textured finish that mimics the look of an elegant wallcovering or fine fabric. This simple technique consists of nothing more than dragging a dry brush vertically through wet glaze that has been applied over a base color. The glaze must be wet for the brush to produce the desired effect in at least two passes from ceiling to floor. If possible, work with a partner. One person can roll on the glaze and the other immediately drags the brush through the glaze. A special dragging brush is available at most paint centers, but a 3- to 4-inch high-quality brush will work as well. For coarser, more pronounced lines, try using a wallpaper brush or even a clean whisk broom. For clean lines, keep plenty of cotton cloths on hand to wipe excess glaze from the brush after each stroke. A strié finish offers a sophisticated look and is well-suited to a more formal decorating scheme. Complementary colors make a strong visual statement. Or use tints and shades of the same color for a subdued effect.

KEEP IT CLEAN
This is a messy technique. Use plenty of waterproof drop cloths to keep your work area paint-free.

1 **DIVIDE THE WALL**
Divide the wall into vertical panels. The panels shown are approximately 3 feet wide. Using a level with printed ruler, measure and mark the panel widths across the wall.

Dragging requires speed and a steady hand after the glaze has been applied to the surface.

2
DRAW VERTICAL LINES
Extend your measurements vertically using a level and colored pencil.

3 **MASK OFF SECTIONS**
Tape off alternating sections with low-tack painter's tape. Burnish the edges of the tape by pressing down hard with your finger to prevent the paint from seeping underneath. To make the glaze, mix 4 parts glaze to 1 part Smokey Slate latex paint in a plastic container. Use a container with printed measurements for ease of measuring.

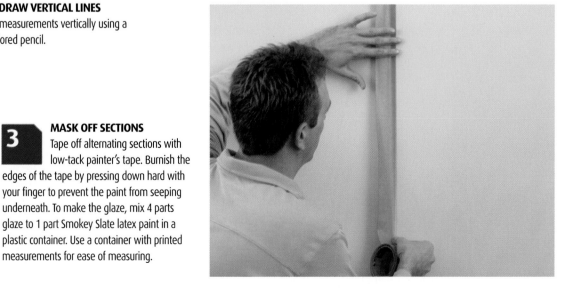

4

DECORATIVE TECHNIQUES

DECORATIVE TECHNIQUES

4

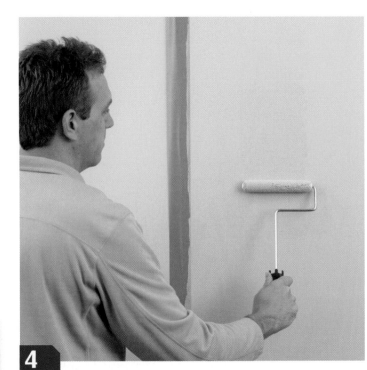

4 **ROLL ON THE GLAZE**

Working quickly, use a trim brush to cut in the ceiling and baseboard with glaze. Roll onto one vertical section using the mini roller. Roll through the glaze a second time to ensure a smooth coat.

 **WORK SMARTER**

PREPARE THE SURFACE
Dragging requires a smooth base. Prepare the wall as shown on pages 40–43 before starting the technique.

5 **DRAG THE BRUSH DOWNWARD**

Starting at the top of the newly glazed section, use a dry, long-bristled brush and drag lightly downward through the wet glaze. Stop the stroke halfway down the wall.

6 **DRAG THE BRUSH UPWARD**

Start the next stroke at the baseboard, pulling upward and gradually lightening the pressure on the brush to meet the unfinished stroke. To create a more interesting pattern, be sure to stagger the stopping points.

 DESIGN TIP

SOFT vs. BOLD
For a softer look, keep light pressure on the brush when dragging. If you desire a bolder look, push firmly against the wall, adding more pressure to the drag.

7 KEEP THE BRUSH CLEAN

Use a clean cloth to wipe excess glaze off the brush after each pass. Complete the panel and allow to dry.

8 MASK OFF THE NEXT PANEL

Tape off the next panel, leaving a narrow section from the previous panel showing. This will ensure a continuous look across the wall. Use the same rolling-and-dragging process until all the panels are completed. Remove all tape and let dry.

GOOD IDEA

RAPID REPAIR
If the effect looks too coarse, you can repair it while the glaze is still wet. Drag the brush through the area a second time. Hold the brush nearly perpendicular to the wall and apply less pressure.

"Strié" is French for striated, describing the fine lines of softly modulated color that you achieve with this technique.

Grass cloth

DECORATIVE TECHNIQUES

4

STUFF YOU'LL NEED

BASE COAT: Grape Green satin finish latex paint

GLAZE COATS: Goldenrod Tea and Burley Wood satin finish latex paints

TOOLS: Drop cloth, paint tray, standard roller frame with 9-inch roller cover, 2-inch tapered trim brush, two 3-inch chip brushes, level with printed ruler, pencil, fine-tip marker, squeegee, crafts knife, 2 plastic containers with printed measurements

MATERIALS: 2-inch low-tack painter's tape, stir sticks, glaze medium, practice board, lint-free cotton cloths

TIME TO COMPLETE

Based on a 12×12 foot room, 8 foot ceiling

EXPERIENCED: 5 hrs.

HANDY: 6.5 hrs.

NOVICE: 8.5 hrs.

BEFORE YOU BEGIN

Prepare the surface according to pages 40–43. Mask the ceiling, baseboards, and trim with low-tack painter's tape. Paint the wall in the Grape Green base-coat color. Paint two coats if necessary. Leave tape on and allow to dry overnight.

Grape Green

Goldenrod Tea

Burley Wood

A grass-cloth finish mimics the look of the popular wallcovering, but gives you the freedom to choose colors that suit your decor. To create the effect, drag a notched squeegee horizontally through wet glaze, allowing the base color to show through. Starting in a corner or beside a doorway provides a straight edge to guide the first pull. Use a shower squeegee for smaller areas such as next to windows and doorways. To alter the look, notch the tool in smaller increments to create finer lines. The wall above uses a dark-colored glaze over a light base coat. For a darker finished appearance, start with a darker background color and apply a light-colored glaze. Closely related neutral colors will give a subtle effect, while browns, greens, and ochers will look naturalistic. Experiment with colors on a practice board to find the effect you like best. Grass cloth works well as a focal point wall or under a chair rail in a casual decorating scheme.

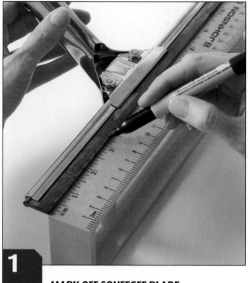

1 MARK OFF SQUEEGEE BLADE
Using a ruler and fine-tip marker, divide the blade of the squeegee into ½-inch sections.

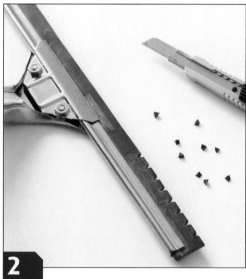

2 CUT OUT ⅛-INCH NOTCHES
With a crafts knife, cut out a small notch about ⅛ inch wide at every mark. Be sure to cut away the ink mark itself to keep the ink from bleeding into the wet glaze.

3 DIVIDE THE WALL INTO SECTIONS
Mark the wall off in 20-inch-wide sections using a level with printed measurements and a pencil. Make a light vertical mark every 20 inches to use as a taping guideline.

4 TAPE OFF VERTICAL SECTIONS
Mask off alternating vertical sections with 2-inch low-tack painter's tape.

DESIGN TIP

STRAIGHT PULLS
Change the effect by varying the width of your panels. Plan sections that are less than 24 inches wide to help keep your horizontal pulls straight.

The grass-cloth effect produces a highly textured pattern that is well-suited for a casual setting.

5 APPLY THE GLAZES

In plastic containers, mix two separate glazes with Goldenrod Tea and Burley Wood, using 4 parts glaze to 1 part paint. Dip the 3-inch chip brush into varying combinations of the glazes. Starting at the top of the wall, brush the glazes onto the first taped-off section with horizontal strokes.

6 DRAG THE SQUEEGEE HORIZONTALLY

While the glaze is wet, place the squeegee on top of the taped edge and drag horizontally until you reach the tape on the opposite edge. Be sure to pull the squeegee onto the tape. Overlap the squeegee pulls by aligning the top notch of the squeegee along a line created by the previous pull, following it across the section. This will help to create a continuous pattern.

7 CLEAN SQUEEGEE WITH A CLOTH

Wipe excess glaze onto a cloth after each pass.

8 SOFTEN THE LINES WITH A BRUSH

Using a dry chip brush, lightly brush the glaze in a horizontal motion to blend and soften the lines. Repeat the process of brushing on glaze, dragging with the squeegee, and dry-brushing to blend until all the taped-off sections are completed. Remove the tape and allow the glaze to dry.

9 MASK OFF UNPAINTED SECTIONS

With painter's tape, outline the remaining sections.

10 **BRUSH ON THE GLAZE IN REMAINING SECTIONS**

Repeat Step 5, brushing on combinations of the two glazes, starting at the top of the wall. Pull the squeegee through the glazed section, then move down the wall, brushing on the glaze with a chip brush. Overlap your brush strokes into the previously glazed section to create a continuous pattern.

11 **PULL SQUEEGEE THOUGH THE GLAZE**

Drag the squeegee horizontally as in Step 6. If the glaze becomes too dry to produce continuous lines, add a small amount of water to the mixtures and reapply the glaze to that section with a chip brush. This will dampen the surface and allow a clean sweep with the squeegee. Soften the lines with the chip brush before the glaze dries. Continue until the alternating sections are completed.

This technique recalls the coarse texture of grass cloth, which is woven from natural plant fibers.

Variation

There are no right or wrong colors for a grass-cloth paint finish. Neutral colors create a subtle look; contrasting colors add more drama. Refer to the color wheel on page 23 and experiment with colors that appeal to you. Hues of blue, green, and brown created the grass-cloth effect on the wall of this sitting room.

4

DECORATIVE TECHNIQUES

Leather

✓ STUFF YOU'LL NEED

BASE COAT: Luster White semigloss finish latex paint
GLAZE COAT: Sunset Beige semigloss finish latex paint
TOOLS: Drop cloth, paint tray, standard roller frame with 9-inch roller cover, 2-inch tapered trim brush, tape measure, level, tan colored pencil, scissors, plastic drop cloth (1 mil thick)
MATERIALS: 2-inch low-tack painter's tape, stir sticks, glaze medium, lint-free cotton cloths

🕐 TIME TO COMPLETE

Based on a 12×12 foot room, 8 foot ceiling
EXPERIENCED: 10 hrs.
HANDY: 12 hrs.
NOVICE: 14 hrs.

↘ BEFORE YOU BEGIN

Prepare the surface according to pages 40–43. Mask the ceiling, baseboards, and trim with painter's tape. Paint the entire wall in the Luster White base-coat color. Paint two coats if necessary. Leave tape on; let dry overnight. Remove ceiling tape.

Luster White

Sunset Beige

Give your walls a rugged, natural finish with the look of leather. The technique uses sheets of plastic to remove wet glaze applied over a dry base-coat color. Working in taped-off rectangular panels allows one person to handle the plastic sheets alone. If you prefer a seamless expanse of leather, you'll need to work with a partner. Have one person cut in and roll on the glaze, and one person cut, shape, and remove the sheets of plastic, keeping the edges irregular to avoid hard lines. Remember that glaze, like paint, darkens as it dries. To achieve the look of natural leather, use tints and shades that are close to one another on the color wheel. As the glaze cures, the difference in hues will become more apparent. Try faux leather in other colors, such as yellow, blue, red, or green, as well as natural browns and tans.

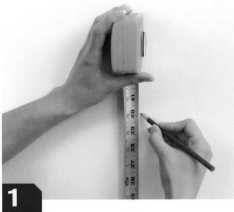

1
MARK THE HORIZONTAL LINES
Divide the wall into sections that you can manage alone, such as 24- to 48-inch-deep panels. Starting at the floor, measure up the wall and mark the divisions.

2
DRAW THE HORIZONTAL LINES
Extend the lines horizontally around the room.

3
MEASURE AND MARK THE VERTICAL LINES
Starting in one corner, measure and mark every 24 to 48 inches or the desired width of your panels.

4
DRAW THE VERTICAL LINES
Extend the lines vertically with the level and colored pencil to complete the rectangular panels.

5
MASK OFF THE SECTIONS
Tape the outside edges of every other rectangle with low-tack painter's tape. Do not tape off the ceiling because glaze will bleed underneath the tape and dry on the ceiling.

4

DECORATIVE TECHNIQUES

GOOD IDEA

A WORK OF ART
Each piece of real leather is visually different. When you apply the plastic onto a section of wet glaze, think of each rectangle as its own individual design or work of art.

Don't limit this finish to walls. Leather can add interest to any flat surface, such as drawer fronts, tabletops, or trunks.

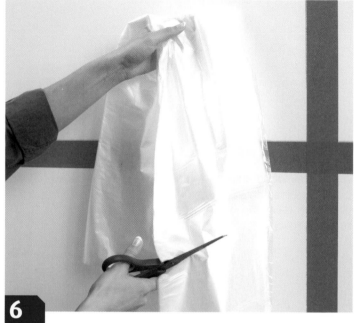

6

CUT PLASTIC INTO SECTIONS
For each panel, cut a piece of plastic drop cloth about a foot longer and wider than the rectangle; set aside. Make a glaze mixture of 4 parts glaze to 1 part Sunset Beige paint in a plastic container. For the wall shown, 1 gallon of glaze was mixed with 1 quart of paint.

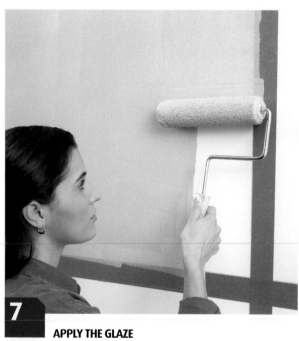

7

APPLY THE GLAZE
Working on one rectangle at a time, roll on the glaze. In the rectangles along the ceiling and baseboard, cut in the glaze along the trim and roll it on over the remainder of the rectangle.

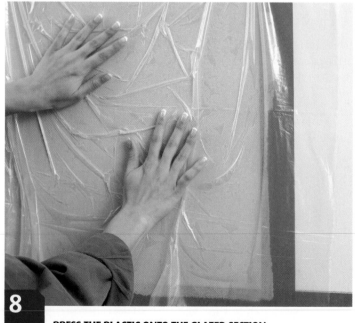

8

PRESS THE PLASTIC ONTO THE GLAZED SECTION
Apply plastic to the glazed section. Avoid dragging your fingers because lines will appear; however, it's fine to leave some fingerprints.

 REMOVE THE PLASTIC
Peel the plastic off, starting at one top corner. Remove tape immediately after removing plastic. If glaze has seeped under the tape, wipe immediately with a damp cloth. Allow to dry. Repeat for the remaining panels.

Variations

This leather effect was created by applying a darker glaze over a light base color. The more you wrinkle the plastic, the more texture you'll achieve. Try a light glaze over a dark base color for a more muted effect.

Be creative with your color choices. Faux leather can come in any color. This room shows a blue faux leather effect. Green and red are other popular colors.

Antique leather

✓ STUFF YOU'LL NEED

BASE COAT: Stadium Red satin finish latex paint
GLAZE COAT: Moroccan Red
TOOLS: Drop cloths, paint trays, standard roller frame with 9-inch roller cover, 2-inch tapered trim brush, Fitch edge tool, stippling brush
MATERIALS: 2-inch low-tack painter's tape, stir sticks, lint-free cotton cloths

🕐 TIME TO COMPLETE

Based on a 12×12 foot room, 8 foot ceiling
EXPERIENCED: 4 hrs.
HANDY: 6 hrs.
NOVICE: 8 hrs.

➲ BEFORE YOU BEGIN

Prepare the surface according to pages 40-43. Mask the ceiling, baseboards, and trim with low-tack painter's tape. Paint the entire wall in the Stadium Red base-coat color. Paint two coats if necessary. Leave tape on and allow to dry overnight.

Stadium red

Achieving the look of aged leather involves a subtractive technique—you roll the glaze onto the wall and then remove it by pouncing the surface with special brushes. If you're an experienced decorative painter, you may want to experiment with mixing your own tinted glaze, but some paint manufacturers take the guesswork out by providing tinted glazes to coordinate with the base coats. That's the case with the glaze used here (see page 185). It's important to glaze adjoining walls on different days to avoid overlapping into areas that have

already been completed. Practice this technique on a piece of scrap board to perfect your technique before starting on a wall. If you can work with a partner, the job will go faster: One person rolls on the strip of glaze, and the second begins stippling immediately. Depending on the colors you choose, you can create a dramatic, elegant statement using shades of blue, green, or red, or a more subtle, natural leather look using shades of brown and gold. Add leather furnishings to further enhance the effect.

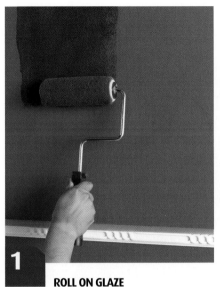

1 **ROLL ON GLAZE**

Starting in the corner of the room, use a standard roller and roll on a single coat of Moroccan Red glaze the width of the roller.

2 **STIPPLE THE GLAZED SECTION**

Quickly begin removing glaze with the stippling brush by tapping the wall with a quick pouncing motion, twisting your wrist back and forth as you pounce. Make sure the stippling brush hits the wall straight on. Continue stippling until you reach the desired effect.

3 **WIPE BRUSH WITH A CLOTH**

Remove excess glaze from the brush with a lint-free cloth after approximately 10 to 15 pounces.

4 **FILL IN HARD-TO-REACH AREAS**

To fill in above trimwork, dip the Fitch edge tool into the glaze and use a pouncing motion to apply a thin layer of glaze to the wall. (Note that you're stippling the glaze onto the wall with this tool, rather than removing it.) Try to match the appearance of the previously stippled area. Use this technique to fill in along the ceiling, in corners, and around door and window frames too.

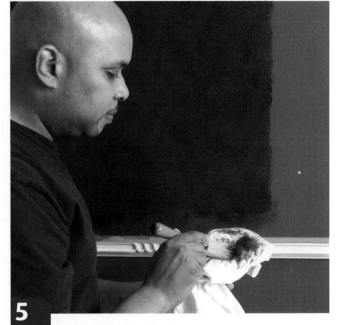

5 **WIPE TOOL WITH A CLOTH**

Wipe excess glaze from the tool with a lint-free cloth. To continue working across the wall, roll on a new strip of glaze, overlapping the previous strip by about 2 inches. Using the stipple brush, first stipple the edge where the new and previously glazed sections meet, blending them together to eliminate visible edges. Then stipple the remainder of the newly glazed section. Use the Fitch edge tool to glaze above trim. Repeat Steps 1-4 until the walls are completed.

Marbleizing

STUFF YOU'LL NEED

BASE COAT: Primer

TOP COATS: Dark Secret, Timber Trail, and Wood Lily satin finish latex paints

TOOLS: Drop cloth, paint tray, 2-inch tapered trim brush, plastic container, scissors, 3-inch chip brush, three 2-inch chip brushes, small artist's brush

MATERIALS: 2-inch low-tack painter's tape, stir sticks, fine-grit sandpaper, tack cloth, plastic (1 mil, cut into several 1×2-foot sections), lint-free cotton cloths, polyurethane

TIME TO COMPLETE

Based on two columns

EXPERIENCED: 6 hrs.

HANDY: 7.5 hrs.

NOVICE: 12 hrs.

BEFORE YOU BEGIN

Prepare the surface according to pages 42. Mask off the area you wish to protect using low-tack painter's tape. Prime the entire surface. Use a fine-grit sandpaper and lightly sand the surface. Wipe off excess dust with a tack cloth.

Dark Secret

Timber Trail

Wood Lily

A lthough marbleizing is a demanding technique, it's a rewarding challenge for decorative painters. It takes experience to achieve the realism of the heavily veined columns above. But with practice, even novices can achieve a convincing marble effect. The secret to the technique is to brush light- and dark-color paints onto pieces of plastic wrap and apply them directly to the surface. Study real marble and, if possible, keep a piece handy when you're painting so you can copy the colors and veining. This effect is ideal for a focal point wall, fireplace surround, columns, wainscoting, and molding, but novices might want to start with a small, flat surface, such as a tabletop, to gain confidence and experience.

1

BRUSH ON THE PAINTS

Determine the direction the marble should flow. For the columns shown, the marble is flowing upward, swirling left to right. Dip the chip brush into the Dark Secret latex paint and then lightly into a container of water. Brush the surface. Repeat this process with the Timber Trail latex paint. Keep the paint thin in some areas and thicker in others for variation.

2

BLEND THE COLORS WITH A CLOTH

While the paint is still wet, use a clean, slightly damp cloth to blend the colors and eliminate any brush strokes. The cloth will leave an impression, adding to the stonelike texture of the marble. Repeat the blending process until the entire surface is completed.

📖 **WORK SMARTER**

GLASSLIKE SURFACE
Before starting this technique, apply at least two coats of primer with a soft brush to create a smooth surface.

3

BRUSH PAINT ONTO PLASTIC

Dip a 2-inch chip brush into various mixtures of Timber Trail and Wood Lily latex paints and brush out onto one of the precut pieces of plastic.

4

APPLY PLASTIC TO THE SURFACE

Lightly place the plastic on the surface, paint side down, following the flow you have created. Let the plastic cling to create random, irregular shapes.

4

DECORATIVE TECHNIQUES

WORK SMARTER

AVOID FINGERPRINTS
Avoid pressing the plastic with your fingertips, or your prints will transfer onto the surface.

5 REPEAT THE PROCESS

Peel the plastic off and shift it to a new area and repeat. You should be able to repeat this process two to four more times before adding more paint. Continue with this step until about 30 percent of the surface is covered. Gently rub the back of the plastic on the final repeat to transfer any remaining paint to the surface.

6 CREATE LIGHT-COLORED VEINS

Dip a small artist's brush (or a feather) into the Wood Lily latex paint and lightly drag it around the light shapes that were created by the plastic application. Vary the veins by adding water to the paint and alternating the pressure of your brush to create light, thin veins or thick, heavy ones. The plastic will not cling in the crevices of the capital and base of the column, so fill in these areas with extra veining. Once you are satisfied with the results, allow to dry.

Depending on the color palette, the final effect can range from a soft, elegant look to a dramatic, classical one.

7 APPLY PLASTIC TO THE SURFACE WITH NEW COLORS

Repeat Steps 3 and 4 with Dark Secret latex paint and Timber Trail latex paint. Brush various mixtures onto a clean piece of plastic and apply it to the surface as before. Avoid going over the areas you've treated with the lighter colors. Remember to allow the plastic's cling to create the shapes. Peel the plastic off and shift it to a new area and repeat.

4

DECORATIVE TECHNIQUES

8 **CREATE DARK-COLORED VEINS**

With a small artist's brush and Dark Secret latex paint, outline and connect the dark shapes. Also incorporate the dark shapes within the lighter areas. Allow to dry. Repeat Steps 3–7 until you achieve the desired results. Let dry completely.

After you achieve a look that pleases you, protect the surface with a coat of polyurethane. A satiny to glossy finish enhances the realism of the marble effect.

Variation

You can create a marble effect in nearly any color. Here, terra-cotta, gold, and brown create a light, rose-marble effect on a focal-point wall. If the finished effect is too dramatic and dark, allow the paint to dry and then wash the entire surface with a thin mixture of white latex paint and glaze to soften and cool down the colors.

Stacked stone

✓ STUFF YOU'LL NEED

BASE COAT: Creme Brulee satin finish latex paint

STONES: Tucson Clay, Clay Earth, and Turtle Shell sandwash paints

TOOLS: Drop cloth, paint tray, standard roller frame with 9-inch roller cover, level with printed ruler, graphite pencil, 3 small plastic paint trays, mini roller frame with 4-inch foam roller cover, 1-inch chip brush

MATERIALS: 1-inch low-tack painter's tape, stir sticks, lint-free cotton cloth

🕐 TIME TO COMPLETE

Based on a 12×12 foot room, 8 foot ceiling

EXPERIENCED: 10 hrs.

HANDY: 13 hrs.

NOVICE: 17 hrs.

◐ BEFORE YOU BEGIN

Prepare the surface according to pages 40–43. Mask the ceiling, baseboards, and trim with painter's tape. Paint the entire wall in the Creme Brulee base-coat color. Paint two coats if necessary. Leave tape on; allow to dry overnight.

Creme Brulee

Tucson Clay

Clay Earth

Turtle Shell

Transform plain walls into an architectural feature with a faux-stone technique. Applying the paint in rectangles of varying sizes produces a stacked-stone effect. This finish uses a textured paint that gives the blocks a slightly rough, sandy surface. (You could also use suede paint or mix a paint texturing material into flat latex paint to achieve a stonelike surface.) To create the effect, plan the design on graph paper first. Keep the blocks large to simplify the design visually and to make the job go more quickly. Then map out the pattern on the wall by taping off the stones with low-tack painter's tape. Mix the textured paint well before and during the painting process to keep the texturing material from settling to the bottom of the can. This effect works best on smooth, nonslick surfaces. Try it in an entryway, stairwell, or around a fireplace.

1   MEASURE AND MARK

Beginning at the top of the wall, mark off 10-inch horizontal guidelines. Use a level to keep your lines straight. Next, mark off 18-inch-wide blocks, randomly staggering them every 6 inches. Selectively divide a few of the blocks horizontally into 4-inch and 6-inch sections.

2   MASK OFF BLOCKS

Tape off non-adjoining blocks with 1-inch low-tack painter's tape.

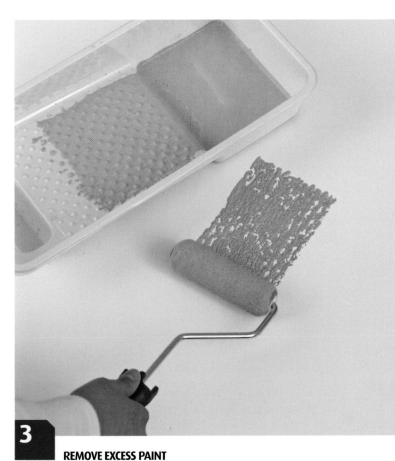

3   REMOVE EXCESS PAINT

Load the foam roller with Tucson Clay. To prevent the pattern on the bottom of the paint tray from transferring onto the wall, lightly roll out twice onto a piece of scrap board.

DESIGN TIP

CHANGE THE LOOK
Instead of dividing some of the blocks into narrower "stones" as shown on the opposite page, keep the stones uniform in size for a more formal look.

Rolling the textured paint in random directions and ragging off areas of color add to the stone finish.

DESIGN TIP

STONE IMITATION
For inspiration, work from photographs in books or magazines that show real stone in a variety of patterns.

4

DECORATIVE TECHNIQUES

4

APPLY THE FIRST COLOR OF PAINT

Lightly roll the Tucson Clay paint onto the taped-off blocks starting along the edge or corner of the block. Allow the paint to go on more heavily in some areas and more lightly in others, but avoid too heavy an application. You can add more paint later if desired, but it is difficult to remove if it's too dark.

5

BLEND WITH A CLOTH

Use a lint-free cotton cloth to dab and blend areas, adding to the stonelike texture. Remove tape and allow to dry. Tape off new blocks and repeat the process with the Tucson Clay paint.

6

VARY THE AMOUNT OF PAINT APPLIED TO EACH BLOCK

Decide which blocks you'll paint the final two colors. Tape off the blocks designated for the Clay Earth paint. Press the tape harder onto the surfaces that have been treated because it will not stick as easily. Roll on the Clay Earth paint in these sections. Experiment with applying the paint more liberally. Emphasize the corners and edges to separate them from the adjacent blocks. Use a lint-free cotton cloth to dab and blend areas. Remove tape and allow to dry.

7

ROLL ON THE FINAL COLOR

Tape off all remaining blocks and roll on the Turtle Shell paint.

8
BLEND WITH A CLOTH
Rag off areas to create a mottled stonelike appearance. Remove tape.

9
OUTLINE THE EDGES
Define edges using Tucson Clay paint and a 1-inch chip brush where desired. Remove all remaining tape. Allow to dry.

Using four related earth tones imitates sandstone and limestone stacked without mortar. For a more uniform look, use only two colors.

4

DECORATIVE TECHNIQUES

Color washing

STUFF YOU'LL NEED

BASE COAT: Cascade White satin finish latex paint
GLAZE COAT: Cinnamon Cherry satin finish latex paint
TOOLS: Drop cloth, paint tray, standard roller frame with 9-inch roller cover, 2-inch tapered trim brush, plastic container with printed measurements
MATERIALS: 2-inch low-tack painter's tape, stir sticks, glaze medium

TIME TO COMPLETE

Based on a 12×12 foot room, 8 foot ceiling
EXPERIENCED: 6 hrs.
HANDY: 7 hrs.
NOVICE: 8 hrs.

BEFORE YOU BEGIN

Prepare the surface according to pages 40–43. Mask the ceiling, baseboards, and trim with low-tack painter's tape. Paint the wall in the Cascade White base-coat color. Paint two coats if necessary. Leave tape on and allow to dry overnight. Mix 4 parts glaze to 1 part Cinnamon Cherry paint in a plastic container with printed measurements. If the mixture appears too heavy, add more glaze. Mix well.

Cascade White

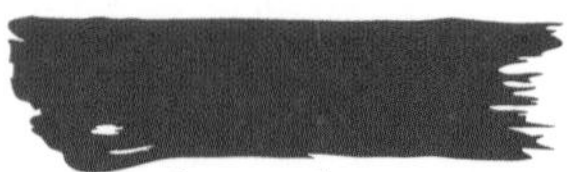

Cinnamon Cherry

Color washing creates a subtle, dimensional finish by blending layers of glaze over a dry base color. The glaze is brushed on using a crosshatching motion. If you are color washing alone, it will be easier to work in panels. Tape off the wall into 3-foot-wide vertical panels and color wash alternating panels. Remove the tape and let the panels dry, then tape off and color wash the remaining panels. Unlike some finishes, color washing can be used on highly textured walls or on surfaces with imperfections as well as on smooth walls. For the effect shown above, a deep-tone top color is washed over a neutral-tone base color. For even more depth, use more than one glaze color. For example, applying two glazes, one mixed with four parts paint to one part glaze and a second of equal parts white paint and glaze, will result in an airy, cloudlike effect. For an aged appearance, use earth tones and apply a darker glaze in the corners, on the ceiling, and around the trim; this simulates the way color tends to bleach over time on the wall surfaces that receive more direct light. Color washing works well with both traditional and contemporary decorating styles and combines easily with other decorative paint techniques, such as stripes, diamonds, and stencils.

1 **CUT IN THE GLAZE**
Using the glaze (see "Before You Begin," page 82) and a 2-inch trim brush, cut in the glaze along the ceiling line and in the corners.

2 **CROSSHATCH THROUGH THE GLAZE**
Working quickly, crosshatch through the glaze randomly, blending the trim lines into the glaze.

3 **COMPLETE ONE WALL**
Continue making Xs as you crosshatch the glaze. Try to complete one section before drying lines appear. After finishing the room, remove all tape and allow the glaze to dry.

Applying a red glaze over a white base yields a mottled finish with pink highlights. The brush strokes are prominent on this wall. If you want a more uniform look, use a barely-damp sponge to "walk" the color over the wall, blending it to eliminate the brush strokes. Rinse the sponge often and wring it nearly dry to avoid removing too much glaze.

Variation

In this bathroom, lighter glaze washed over a darker base coat gives the walls a shimmering quality. After the glaze has been applied randomly, a dry brush is used to soften the contrast.

Graduated color wash

✓ STUFF YOU'LL NEED

BASE COAT: Cottonseed satin finish latex paint

GLAZE COATS: Salted Ash, Acorn, Silk Cypress, Blonde Yellow satin finish latex paints

TOOLS: Drop cloths, four plastic containers with printed measurements, standard roller frame with 9-inch roller cover, 2-inch tapered trim brush, mini roller frame with 6-inch roller cover, 3- to 4-inch good-quality paint brush

MATERIALS: 2-inch low-tack painter's tape, stir sticks, glaze medium, lint-free cotton cloths

🕐 TIME TO COMPLETE

Based on a 12×8-foot focal point wall

EXPERIENCED: 2 hrs.

HANDY: 4 hrs.

NOVICE: 6 hrs.

BEFORE YOU BEGIN

Prepare the surface according to pages 40–43. Mask the ceiling, baseboards, and trim with low-tack painter's tape. Base-coat the entire wall in the Cottonseed paint. Paint two coats if necessary. Leave tape on and allow to dry overnight. Mix four separate glazes using each of the four paint colors in four plastic containers, using 1 part paint to 3 parts glaze.

Cotton Seed

Salted Ash

Acorn

Silk Cypress

Blonde Yellow

Graduated color wash creates an atmospheric watercolor effect. The easiest approach is to use several related colors (here, green, orange, and yellow), but if you like more drama, try imitating the evening sky with lemon fading to canteloupe, cerulean, and deep blue. The colors are simply rolled on horizontally in 2-foot sections and then dry-brushed to blend the edges where two colors meet. The trick is to work quickly to blend the colors before the glaze mixture becomes too dry. Practice on a scrap board first. Because you need to work quickly to achieve the desired effect, consider using graduated color wash in a small room or as a focal point wall. It's best to restrict it to walls with few interruptions, such as windows and doors.

1
ROLL ON THE FIRST COLOR
Using the 6-inch mini roller, roll the Salted Ash glaze horizontally along the bottom of the wall near the baseboard (see "Before You Begin," opposite). Work 2 feet up in the wall in this manner.

2
DRAG WITH A DRY PAINTBRUSH
Drag a dry, 3- to 4-inch good quality paintbrush along the newly glazed section with long, even, horizontal strokes.

3
REMOVE EXCESS GLAZE
Use a lint-free cotton cloth to wipe excess glaze off the brush after each stroke.

4
ROLL ON THE SECOND COLOR
Without cleaning the roller, dip it into the Acorn glaze mixture and roll the glaze onto the wall horizontally, overlapping slightly into the previously glazed section to blend the Salted Ash and Acorn glazes together. Continue 2 feet up the wall with the Acorn glaze.

5
DRAG THE BRUSH HORIZONTALLY
Drag the dry paintbrush along the glazed section, using long horizontal strokes. The goal is to blend the edges where the two glazes meet to eliminate any break in color. Wipe excess glaze off the brush with a lint-free cloth.

6
REPEAT WITH REMAINING COLORS
Dip the roller into the Silk Cypress glaze and repeat the rolling and brushing-out procedure on the next 2-foot section of wall. Complete the remainder of the wall with the Blonde Yellow glaze, rolling and brushing out to the ceiling line.

4

DECORATIVE TECHNIQUES

Whitewashing

✓ STUFF YOU'LL NEED

BASE COAT: Stark White semigloss latex paint

TOOLS: Drop cloth (waterproof), plastic container with printed measurements, 2-inch tapered trim brush

MATERIALS: 2-inch low-tack painter's tape, stir stick, water, lint-free cotton cloths (optional)

🕐 TIME TO COMPLETE

Based on a 12×12 foot room, 8 foot ceiling

EXPERIENCED: 6 hrs.

HANDY: 7 hrs.

NOVICE: 8 hrs.

↻ BEFORE YOU BEGIN

Prepare the surface according to pages 40–43. Mask baseboards and trim with low-tack painter's tape. Mix 1 part white paint with 1 part water in a plastic container. Use a container with printed measurements for easy measuring. Stir well.

Stark White

Whitewashing comes from the old practice of applying a mixture of lime and water to walls. Today you can create this translucent effect by brushing diluted paint onto any raw wood surface. This is a very easy effect to create, but you need to work quickly and wash with the grain of the wood. Wipe with a cotton cloth to reveal more of the natural wood surface. This is a messy technique because of the diluted wash mixture, so you'll need to periodically wipe up any paint spatters, or enlist a partner to clean up as you go. Whitewashing lends itself to a cottage or country decorating scheme. Try it on furniture as well: Paint the piece with diluted white paint, allowing some of the natural wood grain to show through. If desired, randomly sand off some of the paint for a distressed, aged appearance.

1 APPLY THE PAINT
Using a 2-inch tapered trim brush, begin painting in a corner, cutting in the edge and moving out. Paint from top to bottom, moving quickly. If you get wash on an adjoining wall, wipe with a damp cloth and feather the edges with a paintbrush.

2 DAB WITH A COTTON CLOTH
Finish one wall completely before moving to the next wall, or the stopping and starting points will be obvious. If desired, dab with a clean, dry cotton cloth to remove some of the paint, revealing more of the natural wood surface.

 WORK SMARTER

DON'T FORGET TO PREP
Always start with a sanded, clean surface so the paint will adhere to the wall.

3 APPLY A SECOND COAT
Allow the first coat to dry. Add a second coat if desired.

4 ALLOW TO DRY
When all the walls are completed, remove tape; allow to dry.

DESIGN TIP

ALTER THE EFFECT
Try whitewashing in a darker color such as sage green or an even darker color like a mint green. This will give a sheer look with a hint of color. Green will blend nicely with wood tones.

4

DECORATIVE TECHNIQUES

Double rolling

DECORATIVE TECHNIQUES

4

✓ STUFF YOU'LL NEED

BASE COAT, TOP COAT: Wheatfield satin finish latex paint
TOP COAT: Crepe de Chine satin finish latex paint
TOOLS: Drop cloth, paint tray, standard roller frame with 9-inch roller cover, 2-inch tapered trim brush, double roller and extra covers, double-roller tray, 10-in-1-tool
MATERIALS: 2-inch low-tack painter's tape, stir sticks, glaze medium (optional), sea sponge

🕐 TIME TO COMPLETE

Based on a 12×12 foot room, 8 foot ceiling
EXPERIENCED: 4 hrs.
HANDY: 5 hrs.
NOVICE: 6 hrs.

👇 BEFORE YOU BEGIN

Prepare the surface according to pages 40–43. Mask the ceiling, baseboards, and trim with low-tack painter's tape. Paint the wall in the Wheatfield base-coat color. Paint two coats if necessary. Leave tape on and allow to dry overnight.

Wheatfield

Crepe de Chine

Using twin rollers rather than brushes or rags offers beginners an easy way to get a color-washed effect. Double rolling is nearly as fast as rolling on a single color. The only tricky part is cutting in the corners to match the mottled effect on the rest of the wall. One secret to the success of this technique is to forget everything you've learned about not re-rolling over paint—just keep rolling and re-rolling until you have an effect you like. Try the technique on practice boards first to see whether you want to mix the paint with glaze. Working with paint poured from the can, as shown here, will produce an opaque finish. If you mix the paint with glaze, using a ratio of one part paint to four parts glaze, the double-rolled colors will be translucent, allowing some of the base color to show through. For a three-color effect, use a different color for the base and don't completely cover the base coat with the top coat colors. As a general rule, after making color selections, go two shades darker for one glaze and two tints lighter for the other.

1
USE A TRAY WITH TWO CHAMBERS
A double roller requires a matching paint tray with two chambers.

2
FILL THE TRAY CHAMBERS
Fill each tray chamber with a different paint or glaze. Avoid overfilling the chamber. Otherwise, when the roller is dipped into the tray, paint could spill from one chamber into the adjoining one.

The double roller produces an effect similar to color washing in just a fraction of the time.

DECORATIVE TECHNIQUES

4

3
DAMPEN THE ROLLERS
Dampen both roller covers by holding under a tap and squeezing out the excess water. Then fill with paint by rolling carefully in the tray.

4
ROLL PAINTS RANDOMLY ONTO THE SURFACE
Beginning in an upper corner, roll in random directions. Concentrate on getting paint onto the wall rather than covering it completely.

5

CONTINUE ROLLING UNTIL THE SURFACE IS COVERED

After you've applied paint loosely to a 3×4-foot area, continue rolling randomly until the surface is completely covered and the desired effect is attained. Lift the roller between strokes to leave distinct lines; move the roller without lifting it for a more blended look.

6

SCRAPE BUILT-UP PAINT FROM ROLLERS

After rolling approximately four sections, scrape the built-up paint from the rollers using the roller cover scraper on a 10-in-1-tool.

CLOSER LOOK

ROLL, ROLL, ROLL
For a subtle variation in the finish, roll, roll, and reroll over the same spot until you reach the desired results.

7

SPONGE GLAZE IN THE CORNERS

Before the finish dries, use small pieces of sponge to extend the glazes into the corners and any crevices. Use one for each color, and apply the glaze in alternating dabs. (Alternatively, you can sponge the corners first, then quickly blend them with the walls on each side.)

Allow to dry. Remove any remaining tape and allow finish to dry.

DECORATIVE TECHNIQUES

4

Sponging on

✓ STUFF YOU'LL NEED

BASE COAT: Hazelnut Cream satin finish latex paint

GLAZE COATS: Raked Leaves, Dry Sea Grass, and Creme Brulee satin finish latex paints

TOOLS: Drop cloth, three paint trays, standard roller frame with 9-inch roller cover, 2-inch tapered trim brush, plastic container with printed measurements, large sea sponge, small pieces of sea sponge

MATERIALS: 2-inch low-tack painter's tape, stir sticks, water, scrap cardboard

🕐 TIME TO COMPLETE

Based on a 12×12 foot room, 8 foot ceiling

EXPERIENCED: 8 hrs.

HANDY: 10 hrs.

NOVICE: 12 hrs.

↘ BEFORE YOU BEGIN

Prepare the surface according to pages 40–43. Mask the ceiling, baseboards, and trim with low-tack painter's tape. Paint the entire wall in the Hazelnut Cream base-coat color. Paint two coats if necessary. Leave the tape on and allow to dry overnight.

Hazelnut Cream

Raked Leaves

Dry Sea Grass

Creme Brulee

Sponging is one of the easiest techniques you can use to give a wall depth and complexity. Simply pat various colors onto a base-coated wall using a sea sponge. The more colors you sponge on, the greater the illusion of depth. Undiluted paint was used to sponge the wall above, but mixing the top coats with glaze lets you achieve an even softer, more nuanced result because the glaze makes the paint translucent and extends the drying time. As with any technique, practice on a sample board until the desired effect is achieved before starting on the wall. To avoid repeating shapes, rotate the sponge as you move across the wall, or try sponging with alternating hands. Step back and check your work often to ensure a consistent finish. To ensure clean corners, work on opposite walls and mask the adjacent walls at the corners. This lets you work all the way into to the corner with the sponge. This technique is good for hiding flaws on imperfect walls and is a popular treatment for furniture and accessories.

TOOL SAVVY

BY THE SEA
Apply the paint using natural sea sponges, which can be found at most home centers. Try not to squeeze the sponge or push down too hard on the surface. Wash sponges out frequently to prevent them from clogging up with excess paint.

Sponge On, Sponge Off

If you want the base-coat color to be the dominant color on the wall, use the sponging-on technique. If you want less of the base-coat color to show, roll the glaze on and then sponge it off.

1

BRUSH PAINT ONTO THE SPONGE
Wet the sea sponge with water and wring it out thoroughly. Brush Raked Leaves latex paint, or the darkest color, onto the surface of the sponge.

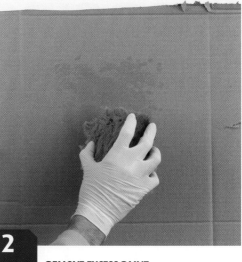

2

REMOVE EXCESS PAINT
Blot excess paint onto a piece of scrap cardboard, if necessary.

Try a monochromatic color scheme to create an effect that's low-contrast but highly sophisticated.

3

APPLY PAINT TO THE WALL
Dab the sponge onto the wall using a light pouncing motion. (You want to "kiss" the wall with the sponge, not press it heavily.) Turn the sponge each time to avoid "footprints" and overlap each impression to completely cover the surface. Apply paint to the corners and around the trim using the small sea sponges. Continue until the wall is covered.

4

APPLY THE SECOND COLOR
Apply Dry Sea Grass latex paint, or the medium color, using the same technique. Sponge corners and around trim last.

5

APPLY THE THIRD COLOR
Sponge Creme Brulee latex paint, or the lightest color, in the same manner. Reapply any of the colors randomly for added dimension until reaching the desired effect. Continue this process until the entire wall is completed.

4

DECORATIVE TECHNIQUES

Ragging off

✓ STUFF YOU'LL NEED

BASE COAT: Shimmer satin finish latex paint

GLAZE COATS: Southern Breeze and Cottonseed satin finish latex paints

TOOLS: Drop cloth, paint trays, standard roller frame with 9-inch roller cover, 2-inch tapered trim brush, plastic container with printed measurements, mini roller frame with 6-inch roller cover

MATERIALS: 2-inch low-tack painter's tape, stir sticks, glaze medium, lint-free cotton cloths

🕐 TIME TO COMPLETE

Based on a 12×12 foot room, 8 foot ceiling

EXPERIENCED: 8 hrs.

HANDY: 10 hrs.

NOVICE: 12 hrs.

⊘ BEFORE YOU BEGIN

Prepare the surface according to pages 40–43. Mask the ceiling, baseboards, and trim with low-tack painter's tape. Paint the wall in the Shimmer base-coat color. Paint two coats if necessary. Leave tape on and allow to dry overnight.

Shimmer

Southern Breeze

Cottonseed

Ragging off introduces a mottled texture similar to sponging but softer. To achieve this finish, roll glaze over a base-coat color and then quickly remove it with a damp cotton cloth. Reshaping the cloth can produce an assortment of textures. Before starting on a wall, practice shaping the cloth and removing glaze from a sample board until the desired pattern is achieved. A variety of cotton cloths will work for this technique, including old T-shirts, cotton painter's rags, or cheesecloth. Ragging off is the perfect finish to hide rough or uneven wall surfaces. To achieve the merest hint of texture, select colors that are close together on the color wheel. Choose contrasting colors for a more dramatic result.

WORK SMARTER

GIVE IT A SPRAY

Thinning the glaze with water or a latex paint conditioner will keep the glaze workable for a longer period. If you need to touch up a spot after the glaze has dried, simply mist the spot with a spray bottle of water. The water reactivates the glaze for touch-up.

1 ROLL ON THE GLAZE

Mix 1 part Southern Breeze latex paint to 4 parts glaze medium in a plastic container. Roll glaze onto the wall, keeping the area irregular-shaped with uneven edges. Work in a section approximately 3×3 feet.

2 DAB WITH A CLOTH

Immediately soften the edges of the working area with a clean, damp cloth. This will allow the areas to blend together evenly. Be sure to change cloths often.

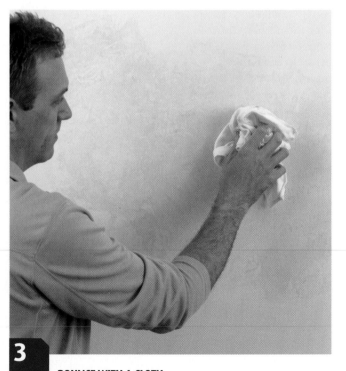

3 POUNCE WITH A CLOTH

Use a pouncing motion with a cloth to allow some of the base-coat color to show through. Reshape and rotate the rag often to avoid a "footstep" pattern within the working area.

4 **ROLL ON SECOND GLAZE**
Mix 1 part Cottonseed latex paint to 4 parts glaze medium in a plastic container. Use the 6-inch mini roller and roll the glaze onto the wall in random areas, keeping the area irregular shaped with uneven edges.

5 **DAB WITH A CLOTH**
Soften and blend the edges by dabbing with a clean, damp cloth as in Step 2.

Ragging on

Ragging on creates a more mottled finish than the subtle ragging-off effect. Start with smooth walls; this technique won't hide dents, cracks, or holes in the surface. Apply the base-coat color and let it dry. Soak a cloth in the glaze mixture; wearing gloves, squeeze out the excess glaze, wad or roll the cloth, and press it to the wall. Use a light tapping motion to create a random pattern. Repeat with a second glaze mixture.

6 **REPEAT THE PROCESS**
Move to a new section and repeat the same process. Blend each completed area into the new section to avoid hard lines. Continue this process until the wall is completed. Remove all tape; allow to dry.

4

DECORATIVE TECHNIQUES

Aging

✓ STUFF YOU'LL NEED

BASE COAT, TOP COAT: Canvasback flat finish latex paint

TOP COATS: Clove and Manuscript flat finish latex paints

TOOLS: Drop cloth, mini paint trays, standard roller frame with 9-inch roller cover, 2-inch tapered trim brush, 4-inch chip brush, sea sponges (large and small), plastic container of water, 2- and 6-inch plastic trowels, plastic container with printed measurements

MATERIALS: 2-inch low-tack painter's tape, stir sticks, glaze medium

🕐 TIME TO COMPLETE

Based on a 12×12 foot room, 8 foot ceiling

EXPERIENCED: 8 hrs.

HANDY: 10.5 hrs.

NOVICE: 13.5 hrs.

◑ BEFORE YOU BEGIN

Prepare the surface according to pages 40–43. Mask the ceiling, baseboards, and trim with painter's tape. Paint the entire wall in the Canvasback base-coat color. Leave tape on; let dry overnight.

Canvasback

Clove

Manuscript

Aging is a popular effect that gives walls the illusion of a timeworn, textured finish. Paints are applied using a brush and trowel and then blended with a damp sea sponge. When applying the paint, avoid flattening the trowel but allow it to catch on the surface, depositing the paint. Use small pieces of sea sponge to blend in the corners and along the ceiling and trimwork. This look can range anywhere from subtle aging to a heavily worn finish. Practice right on the wall—the more variation you add to the surface, the more authentic the final result. Choose similar colors for a subtle effect and contrasting colors for more drama. If you end up with more contrast than you like, simply sponge on a watered-down wash of a dark or light neutral color to help pull the tones together and unify the surface. This effect works well in an entryway, bedroom, dining room, or living room.

1 BRUSH ON PAINT

Dip a 4-inch chip brush into the Clove latex paint and brush onto the surface of the wall.

2 BLEND USING A SEA SPONGE

Wet the sea sponge and squeeze out any excess water. Blend the Clove paint with the damp sponge, using a dabbing motion and feathering the edges. Continue to apply the Clove in selected spots, leaving some areas heavy, and others light.

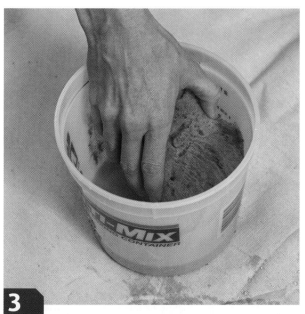

3 RINSE THE SPONGE IN WATER

Rinse your sponge occasionally, squeezing out excess water.

4 DIP THE TROWEL INTO THE SECOND PAINT

Dip the edge of a 6-inch plastic trowel into a mini paint tray of Manuscript latex paint.

Now.

OLD WORLD | AGING *(continued)*

4 DECORATIVE TECHNIQUES

5 APPLY RANDOMLY, USING SWEEPING MOTIONS
Apply to the wall in long, sweeping motions, reloading your trowel as often as necessary. Vary the direction you apply the paint to give it a random, inconsistent look. Allow the paint on the trowel to catch on the surface of the wall rather than pressing the trowel firmly to the surface. This will give the paint a spotty, weathered appearance. Use the smaller trowels in hard-to-reach areas.

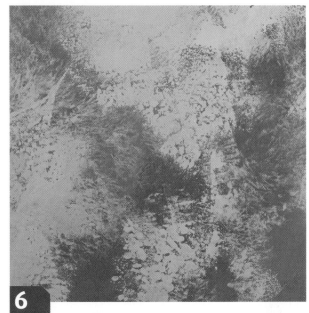

6 CONTINUE TROWELING ON PAINT
Trowel on the Manuscript until you are satisfied with the results.

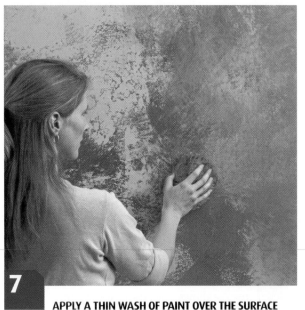

7 APPLY A THIN WASH OF PAINT OVER THE SURFACE
Mix 4 parts glaze to 1 part Canvasback in a plastic container. Dip a clean, damp sea sponge into the glaze mixture and apply a thin wash of paint over the entire surface. Vary your application by using wiping and dabbing motions. Leave the glaze heavier in some areas and thinner in others.

8 CONTINUE APPLYING THE GLAZE MIXTURE
Apply the glaze mixture with the sea sponge until you are satisfied with the results.

9

APPLY PAINT TO SELECT AREAS

Dip a clean 6-inch trowel into the Clove latex paint. Apply it to the wall in the same manner as the Manuscript. Be selective about how much and where you apply it. Emphasize areas that naturally show more aging, such as near the bottom of the walls, next to a window or doorway, or in the corners near the ceiling.

10

SOFTEN THE DARK EDGES

Dip the clean, slightly damp sea sponge into the Canvasback and sponge on using a dabbing motion. Apply this coat sparingly. Use this layer to soften the edges of the Clove.

11

ADD HIGHLIGHTS

Repeat Step 9 using Manuscript, applying it only where needed to create more drama or add highlights. Allow to dry and remove any remaining tape. Allow to dry completely.

Troweling layers of undiluted paint onto the wall produces a richly textured backdrop that suits both traditional and modern interiors.

Aged wallpaper

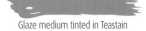

Glaze medium tinted in Teastain

Refurbish a favorite wallcovering with a vintage look. To age wallpaper, simply roll on a tinted glaze using vertical strokes and soften by ragging gently with a lint-free cloth. Be careful not to remove too much glaze. A uniform coating should remain on the wallpaper. Use a specialized tool called a Fitch edging brush to apply glaze to tight areas, such as corners and along the ceiling and trim. This technique works well when the glaze is applied in vertical strips. Avoid overlapping the glaze into adjacent sections, but instead use a cloth to blend the two sections together. For a weathered appearance, leave some areas, such as around doorways, darker. Test the glaze on a small piece of wallpaper before starting on the wall. Darker tints like the one used in the room above add a timeworn atmosphere. Lighter tints provide a faded look. The aging technique can also be applied to painted surfaces.

1 **ROLL ON GLAZE**
Soak the roller in glaze and apply evenly in vertical strips approximately 16 inches wide.

2 **DAB WITH A CLOTH**
Gently dab the surface with a lint-free cotton cloth to lighten the glaze. Turn the cloth occasionally so it continues to absorb the glaze. Avoid ragging the vertical edges—keep them wet to blend in the next vertical strip.

3

DIP THE BRUSH IN GLAZE

Dip the tip of the Fitch edge tool into the pan of glaze, being careful not to overload the brush. If this happens, wipe the excess with a cloth.

4

APPLY GLAZE TO TIGHT AREAS

Use the tool to reach tight areas such as corners, along the trim edges, and along the ceiling lines, using a pouncing or stippling motion.

5

ALLOW TO DRY

Continue down the wall until completed. Remove all tape and allow glaze to dry.

Variations: Compare the effects

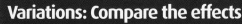

This wall shows the aging effect on black-and-white toile wallpaper. Only the left side of this wallpaper has been aged. Notice the darker, vintage effect on the side that was treated with the brown-tinted glaze.

The faded wallpaper technique uses a light-tinted glaze to simulate the fading effects of the sun. Apply using the same procedure as the Aged Wallpaper finish. Concentrate the effect opposite windows or on areas that may receive additional fading from the sun. Experiment on a practice board until you are satisfied with the results.

4

DECORATIVE TECHNIQUES

Faux Venetian plaster

✓ STUFF YOU'LL NEED

BASE COAT, TOP COAT: Wood Lily flat finish latex paint

TOP COATS: Seahorse, Haymarket, Creme Brulee flat finish latex paints

TOOLS: Drop cloth, 6-inch plastic trowel, four 7-inch plastic paint trays

MATERIALS: 2-inch low-tack painter's tape, stir sticks, lint-free cotton cloths

🕐 TIME TO COMPLETE

Based on a 12×12 foot room,
8 foot ceiling

EXPERIENCED: 7 hrs.

HANDY: 9 hrs.

NOVICE: 12 hrs.

🔄 BEFORE YOU BEGIN

Prepare the surface according to pages 40–43. Mask ceiling, baseboards, and trim with low-tack painter's tape. Paint the entire wall in the Wood Lily base-coat color. Leave tape on; let dry overnight.

Wood Lily

Seahorse

Haymarket

Creme Brulee

Mimic the timeworn look of a plastered wall by applying layers of undiluted paint with a trowel. The paint layers give the wall a textured look that is actually smooth to the touch. Start at the top of the wall and work down toward the floor. Watch for drips that run down the surface and smooth them out immediately before they dry. Once the paint begins to dry and the trowel scratches the surface, move to a new area and come back after the paint has dried completely. Add more tones and highlights as desired. Although this technique can be done on any surface, it's best to apply it to a flat, smooth one. Fill holes and sand the wall completely to prevent the trowel from catching on bumps and in crevices, creating streaks while you're pulling the trowel across the surface. Experiment on a practice board before moving to the wall. This will also provide an opportunity to try out an array of paint colors. Consider colors of varying intensity. This finish is effective in almost any size space, such as entryways, dining rooms, living rooms, or even baths.

1 APPLY PAINTS TO THE TROWEL

Pour Wood Lily, Seahorse, Haymarket, and Creme Brulee latex paints into separate paint trays. Dip the trowel into the Creme Brulee latex paint and then immediately into the Haymarket latex paint.

2 TROWEL ON PAINTS

Starting at the top of the wall, trowel on the paint using vertical and horizontal motions. Continue to dip the trowel into various color combinations of all four colors as you build layers. Apply darker colors to the top edges and corners for a more authentic aged look.

 TOOL SAVVY

BLEND AS YOU GO
Use a lint-free cotton cloth to further soften and blend selected areas as you work.

3 SMOOTH OUT DRIPS OF PAINT

Watch for drips on the lower section of the wall and smooth them out before they dry.

4 ADD HIGHLIGHTS OF THE LIGHTEST COLOR

Occasionally apply Wood Lily alone using light pressure and skipping the trowel across the surface. Holding the trowel perpendicular to the surface as you drag it across the surface will leave more dramatic deposits of paint.

DECORATIVE TECHNIQUES

4

5

DRAG THE TROWEL IN ALL DIRECTIONS

Use vertical and horizontal dragging motions, varying your pulls from left to right and right to left as you add layers of color. Avoid overworking an area. As the paint dries it will become unworkable, so move on to another area. After a section dries, come back to it if you aren't happy with the results.

6

APPLY FINAL HIGHLIGHTS

When you are satisfied with an area, make a final application of pure Wood Lily for highlights.

7

REPEAT THE PROCESS

Continue to work across the wall. After you have completed the entire wall, step back and evaluate the effect. Add more deep tones and highlights as desired. Remove tape and allow to dry.

Variation

The faux Venetian plaster finish in this dining room uses gold, brown, and green hues to achieve an old-world plastered effect. A final wash of thin brown glaze softens and unifies the colors. For a crisp accent, paint trim in solid off-white gloss or semigloss paint.

Venetian plaster

STUFF YOU'LL NEED

BASE COAT: New Penny satin finish latex paint

TOOLS: Drop cloth (waterproof), paint tray, standard roller frame with 9-inch roller cover, 2-inch tapered trim brush, mud pan, 6-inch flexible steel plaster blade

MATERIALS: 2-inch low-tack painter's tape, stir sticks, Venetian plaster tinted in Tuscan Villa, practice wallboard, 400- or 600-grit sandpaper, lint-free cotton cloths, Venetian plaster top coat

TIME TO COMPLETE

Based on a 12×12 foot room, 8 foot ceiling
EXPERIENCED: 12hrs.
HANDY: 13 hrs.
NOVICE: 16 hrs.

BEFORE YOU BEGIN

Prepare the surface according to pages 40–43. Mask ceiling, baseboards, and trim with low-tack painter's tape. Prime or paint the surface using the New Penny base-coat color. Apply two coats if necessary. Leave tape on and allow to dry overnight.

New Penny

Tuscan Villa

Venetian plaster is an old-world wall treatment that gives walls a silky smooth finish with a slightly marbled appearance. Venetian plaster is mostly binder with a small amount of tint. You don't need to lavish it on the wall—just two sheer coats will do the job. Round the corners of the trowel with a file to avoid leaving straight lines in the plaster. Burnishing the plastered wall with a palm sander smooths uneven edges and polishes the surface. Or you can skip the burnishing step and apply the specially formulated top coat, which makes the finish durable enough for kitchens, bathrooms, and high-traffic areas. For an aged effect, mix a few drops of raw umber paint into the top coat; for subtle sparkle, mix in metallic or pearlescent paint. Venetian plaster is ideal for covering cracks or imperfections on a wall or using on a surface that was previously wallpapered. You can have Venetian plaster tinted in any color you like, but keep in mind, the darker the color, the more variation in finish, and the lighter the color, the softer the look.

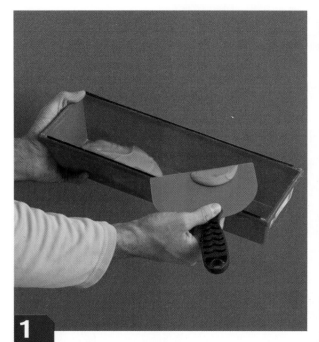

1

PLACE PLASTER ON THE BLADE

Place a small portion of premixed plaster into a mud pan. Use a flexible metal plaster blade and practice applying plaster to a piece of scrap wallboard. Place a thin strip of plaster on the rim of the blade. Wipe excess plaster off the blade using the angled sides of the mud pan.

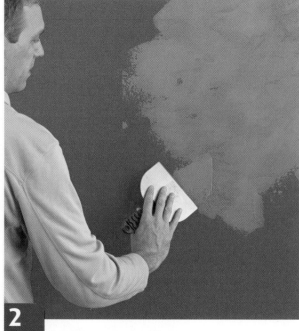

2

APPLY PLASTER TO THE WALL

Start in an upper corner of the wall and work diagonally and downward. Holding the blade at a low angle to the wall, deposit the material from the blade onto the wall, pulling and spreading plaster across the surface with short, random strokes. This will leave a thin, smooth coat of plaster. Allow some of the original wall surface to show through the first coat. Repeat to cover the wall.

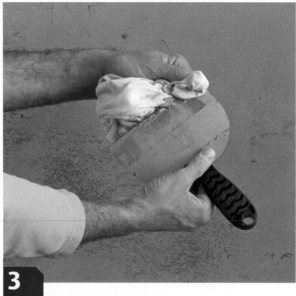

3

KEEP THE TROWEL CLEAN

Use a clean, damp cloth to frequently wipe off your trowel to prevent the plaster from building up on the tool. When the first coat is finished, allow to dry overnight.

4

APPLY A SECOND COAT

Apply a second thin coat of plaster using short, random strokes that slightly overlap. When finished, allow to dry for 24 hours before burnishing or top coating.

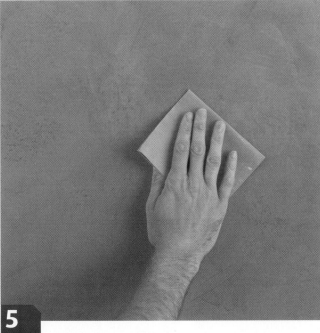

5

BURNISH WITH SANDPAPER

Using a circular motion, burnish with 400- or 600-grit sandpaper to smooth any uneven areas. (You can also burnish the surface using a palm sander, replacing the sandpaper with a piece of paper bag.) Remove dust with a damp cloth.

6

RUB THE BLADE AGAINST THE WALL

For a glossy finish, use the flat side of a clean blade and rub it against the wall in a crisscross pattern. Move across the entire wall until completed. Apply a coat of paste wax if desired.

7

OR SKIP THE BURNISHING AND APPLY THE TOP COAT

For high-moisture and high-traffic areas, skip the burnishing step and apply a protective coating of Venetian plaster top coat. Use a 4-inch or larger steel trowel to pull and spread a thin layer across the wall. Hold the trowel at an angle while you pull and spread. The top coat will darken the finish.

Variation

VENETIAN PLASTER WITH STENCIL

Add a raised design to your Venetian plaster wall with a single overlay stencil. Base-coat the wall using Tuscan Tan latex paint. Apply one thin layer of Venetian plaster tinted in Cottonseed and let dry. Position the stencil template on the wall and tape corners with low-tack painter's tape. Trowel on a thin layer of plaster over the stencil design. Allow to dry for five minutes and carefully pull off the stencil. Apply two more thin layers of Tuscan Tan over the entire wall, including the stenciled areas. Let dry. Sand the stenciled area with 400-grit sandpaper to bring out more color.

Rustic

✓ STUFF YOU'LL NEED

BASE COAT: Bavarian Cream satin finish latex paint

GLAZE COATS: Chestnut Stallion and Wooden Cabin satin finish latex paints

TOOLS: Drop cloth, 6-inch metal plaster knife, paint tray, standard roller frame with 9-inch roller cover, two 4-inch paintbrushes, two plastic containers with printed measurements, cheesecloth

MATERIALS: 2-inch low-tack painter's tape, stir sticks, primer, drywall joint compound, glaze medium

🕐 TIME TO COMPLETE

Based on a 12×12 foot room, 8 foot ceiling

EXPERIENCED: 12 hrs.

HANDY: 14 hrs.

NOVICE: 16 hrs.

🖌 BEFORE YOU BEGIN

Mask ceiling, baseboard, and trim with low-tack painter's tape.

Bavarian Cream

Chestnut Stallion

Wooden Cabin

This textured effect is created with joint compound, producing a stuccolike appearance. Look for a joint compound with a slow setting time; premixed compound may be too brittle when it dries and will chip. When applying, use a plaster knife or trowel and place a generous portion on the wall. Don't try to be neat; the rougher the application, the better the overall finish. Remember that the final effect should be three-dimensional. When the compound is dry, use a brush and apply the glazes. Use your trowel to move the glazes around and fill in all the crevices. Soften the brush strokes and blend the glaze colors together with cheesecloth, rotating the cloth often to find a clean, dry area. When the cloth becomes saturated, change to a new cloth. This rustic effect is ideal for giving imperfect walls an old-world look. Try it in a kitchen, dining room, sunroom, entryway, or as a focal point wall.

1 APPLY COMPOUND TO THE WALL

Apply a generous portion of joint compound with a plaster knife. Working in a section approximately 3×3 feet, apply compound to the wall using a sweeping motion in an overlapping, random pattern. The finish should be rough and uneven. Continue across the wall, working in 3×3-foot sections until completed. Allow to dry overnight.

WORK SMARTER

WORKABLE PLASTER
To help make plaster or joint compound workable, add a small amount of water and mix thoroughly. This will allow more time to smear the plaster until you reach the desired effect.

2 PRIME THE WALL

Using the standard roller frame and 9-inch roller cover, apply primer to the entire wall.

3 FILL IN AREAS THAT AREN'T COVERED

Use a 4-inch brush to fill in areas that the roller doesn't cover. Allow the primer to dry approximately four hours.

4

DECORATIVE TECHNIQUES

4

DECORATIVE TECHNIQUES

4

APPLY THE BASE COAT

Paint the entire wall in the Bavarian Cream base coat. Apply two coats if necessary.

5

FILL IN WITH A BRUSH

Use a brush to fill in areas that weren't completely covered by the roller. Allow to dry approximately 4 hours.

6

BRUSH ON THE GLAZE

Mix 4 parts glaze to 1 part Chestnut Stallion in a plastic container. Working in a 3×3-foot section and using a crisscross motion, start at the top of the wall and brush on the Chestnut Stallion glaze.

7

BRUSH ON SECOND GLAZE

Mix 4 parts glaze to 1 part Wooden Cabin in a second container. Brush on Wooden Cabin glaze randomly within the 3×3-foot section.

8

DAB WITH A CLOTH
Soften and blend the two colors by dabbing with a clean, dry cheesecloth. Slightly soften the edges so the working areas blend into one unified section.

9

REPEAT THE PROCESS
Move to the next 3×3-foot section and repeat Steps 6–8. When the entire wall is finished, remove all tape and allow to dry overnight.

The combination of joint compound and glazes gives the finished wall both literal and illusionistic texture and depth.

CLOSER LOOK

THREE-DIMENSIONAL EFFECT
Walls with texture will collect more glaze and give the surface a three-dimensional illusion.

TOOL SAVVY

SHAKE IT OUT
Shake the cheesecloth before using it to remove loose fibers and threads.

Texture

✓ STUFF YOU'LL NEED

BASE COAT: Honey Tone satin finish latex paint

GLAZE COAT: Corn Husk Green flat finish latex paint

TOOLS: Drop cloth, paint trays, two standard roller frames with 9-inch thick-nap roller covers, mini roller frame with 6-inch foam roller, 2-inch tapered trim brush, 6-inch plastic trowel, plastic container with printed measurements

MATERIALS: 2-inch low-tack painter's tape, stir sticks, smooth texture paint, glaze medium, lint-free cotton cloths

⏱ TIME TO COMPLETE

Based on a 12×12 foot room,
8 foot ceiling

EXPERIENCED: 14 hrs.

HANDY: 16.5 hrs.

NOVICE: 19.5 hrs.

✎ BEFORE YOU BEGIN

Prepare the surface according to pages 40–43. Repair large holes and cracks. (Small imperfections are fine to leave.) Mask ceiling, baseboards, and trim with low-tack painter's tape.

Honey Tone

Corn Husk Green

Texture paint adds depth and dimension to walls, and it's a great way to hide small imperfections. In fact, repair only large holes and cracks, because smaller imperfections will be covered up with the paint. If you are painting over a glossy surface, de-gloss the surface first, following the instructions on page 41. The paint is easy to apply with a thick-nap roller. The more texture you add to the wall, the more dramatic the final effect. Use a trowel to shift the paint, leaving the surface uneven, with areas smooth in some places and rougher in others. When the paint is dry, brush on various glaze mixtures to add more intensity to the wall. Blend the glazes with a damp rag, removing some glaze for stronger definition. Change the shape of the rag often to leave a variety of impressions. For a subtle effect, try colors that are close to each other on the paint strip that includes your chosen color; for a richer, bolder look, use contrasting colors from different paint chips. This finish is durable for most areas, such as living rooms, dining rooms, kitchens, hallways, and baths. Also try this effect in a garden room.

1
APPLY TEXTURE PAINT

Using a thick-nap roller, apply the smooth texture paint, beginning at the top of the wall and working downward. Vary your motions, rolling vertically, horizontally, and on the diagonal. Allow the texture to go on thickly in some areas and lightly in others. Work in approximately 3×3-foot sections until completed.

2
TROWEL THE SURFACE

While the paint is still wet, trowel or knock down the surface of the texture, smoothing out heavier areas and leaving some rough. Wipe the trowel with a cloth occasionally to prevent dried particles from leaving scratches. Repeat until you have worked over the entire surface. Go back and apply more paint to some areas, dipping the trowel directly into the texture paint and skipping it across the surface. The more texture you build, the more dramatic the glaze will appear. Allow to dry completely.

3
APPLY BASE COAT

With a thick-nap roller, apply the Honey Tone base color to the entire textured surface. Apply two coats if necessary. Allow to dry.

4 ROLL ON THE GLAZE

Mix 1 part Corn Husk Green latex paint to 3 parts glaze medium in a plastic container. Use a mini roller to apply the glaze in small sections at a time, approximately 3×3 feet.

5 WORK THE GLAZE INTO THE CREVICES

Work the glaze into the texture with a clean, slightly damp cotton cloth. Turn the cloth as you go. Keep a wet edge to avoid distinct lines as you glaze from one section to another. Rinse out the rag occasionally and lightly lift off the glaze to reveal stronger highlights and more definition. Continue until the entire surface is glazed. Remove the tape and allow to dry.

Textured paint provides dimension to the surface. Colors will appear lighter in flat areas and deeper in the crevices, enhancing the overall depth.

Smooth texture paint creates an effect similar to the Rustic technique but is not as coarse and rough.

Vertical stripes

STUFF YOU'LL NEED

BASE COAT: Cucumber Crush satin finish latex paint

STRIPE: Rockwood Jade satin finish latex paint

TOOLS: Drop cloth, paint tray, standard roller frame with 9-inch roller cover, 2-inch tapered trim brush, level with printed ruler, green colored pencil, mini roller frame with 4-inch roller cover

MATERIALS: 2-inch low-tack painter's tape, stir sticks

TIME TO COMPLETE

Based on a 12×12 foot room, 8 foot ceiling

EXPERIENCED: 10 hrs.

HANDY: 12 hrs.

NOVICE: 14 hrs.

BEFORE YOU BEGIN

Prepare the surface according to pages 40–43. Mask ceiling, baseboards, and trim with low-tack painter's tape. Paint the wall in the Cucumber Crush base-coat color. Paint two coats if necessary. Leave tape on and allow to dry overnight.

Cucumber Crush

Rockwood Jade

Vertical stripes are one of the most versatile wall finishes. They complement any decorating style, from sophisticated and sleek to casual and relaxed, depending on the width of the stripes and the colors selected. Choose narrow, high-contrast stripes for small rooms to draw the eye upward, giving the space a feeling of airiness. Try neutral-color wide stripes to visually expand tight spaces. Tone-on-tone stripes provide a more subtle effect, adding warmth and interest. Hand-painted stripes add a whimsical, casual look. Stripes can also be sponged or ragged to add a touch of depth and dimension. Before painting, sketch the design on paper to help you visualize the pattern. After applying the base color and drawing the lines for the stripes, make an X with painter's tape on the stripes that will remain in the base color. That will help you know at a glance which stripes to tape off for painting. Remove the tape as soon as you finish applying the final coat of paint to prevent lifting the new paint.

DESIGN TIP

SHINY AND FLAT

Instead of striping a room in two different colors, try using the same color in two finishes—flat or satin combined with high-gloss, for example. The glossy/matte contrast adds dimension and interest to the walls while preserving the unifying effect of a single color.

1 MEASURE HORIZONTALLY

Start at the top of the wall and mark every 5 inches with the colored pencil, moving horizontally across the wall. Start measuring opposite the least-seen corner and continue around the room. Allow the stripe to fold around the corner, or adjust your measurements as necessary to end with a stripe in the corner. If you are striping a room with four adjoining walls, measure the last 4 feet of the wall and adjust the stripe widths to fit the space. Continue the pattern, making certain that you end with the appropriate colored stripe.

TOOL SAVVY

LASER STRAIGHT

Make quick work of drawing the lines for stripes with a laser level. Available for as little as $20, this tool attaches to the wall with a suction cup and shoots a beam of light along the surface, eliminating the need to measure and mark with ruler and carpenter's level.

2 DRAW VERTICAL LINES

Extend each stripe vertically with the level and colored pencil. Choose a pencil that closely matches the wall color.

WORK SMARTER

STRIPE TRICKS

If you think your walls might not be perfectly square, start the first stripe in the center of the wall and work toward the corners. Any imperfections will be less noticeable. If your walls are fairly square, start in the corners with a half-width stripe on each side and work toward the center of each wall. The stripes will wrap the room like a gift box.

3 MASK OFF

Tape off using low-tack painter's tape along the outside edges of the marks. Press down firmly on the inner edges of the tape. You will appear to have two widths of stripes. The wider stripe is the one that should be painted. Make a light X on the stripes that should remain in the base-coat color, if desired.

4 REPAINT THE BASE COLOR

Repaint the base coat of the wall color onto the stripe to prevent the Rockwood Jade paint from bleeding underneath the tape.

5 APPLY THE STRIPE COLOR

After the base coat dries, apply the first coat of Rockwood Jade latex paint with the mini roller. After the first coat dries, apply a second coat if necessary. Remove tape. Continue painting stripes until the entire room is completed. Carefully remove all remaining tape as soon as the last coat of paint is applied.

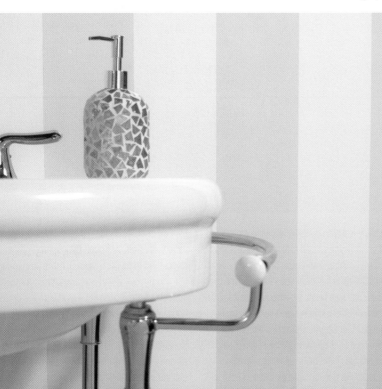

 DESIGN TIP

CHANGE THE LOOK
Try varying the stripe widths for added interest. The darker green stripes could be 5 inches each with 7 inches in between, or try a random pattern and vary the stripe widths from 6 to 15 inches.

Vertical stripes make a small room feel more expansive by leading your eye up to the ceiling. The contrasting colors also create an illusion of depth because the stronger color seems to advance while the lighter color recedes.

DECORATIVE TECHNIQUES

4

Metallic horizontal stripes

STUFF YOU'LL NEED

BASE COAT: Stonegate metallic paint
LARGE STRIPES: Turquoise Sea metallic paint
SMALL STRIPES: Ambassador Sterling metallic paint
TOOLS: Drop cloth, 4½-inch metallic roller frame and cover, mini paint tray, 9-inch metallic roller frame and cover, standard paint tray, level with printed ruler, black fine-tip marker
MATERIALS: 2-inch low-tack painter's tape, stir sticks, latex primer, 1-inch low-tack painter's tape

TIME TO COMPLETE

Based on a 12×12 foot room, 8 foot ceiling
EXPERIENCED: 10 hrs.
HANDY: 11.5 hrs.
NOVICE: 14 hrs.

BEFORE YOU BEGIN

Prepare the surface according to pages 40–43. Mask the ceiling, baseboards, and trim with 2-inch painter's tape.

Stonegate

Turquoise Sea

Ambassador Sterling

Give a shiny luster to walls by applying a metallic paint finish. A specialized roller is used to apply the paint, giving the surface a hammered-metal look. The first coat of paint will appear uneven; a second coat should be applied for an even finish. Geometric designs such as stripes, diamonds, or blocks emphasize a contemporary style. When masking off for geometric motifs, adhere the tape outside the marked lines so they will be covered up when the top coat is applied. Metallic paints can combine with other decorative paint finishes such as sponging or ragging for a shimmery, luminous effect. Or try an antique

look on doors or molding. Metallic paints come in a large variety of colors. Although they reflect light, even the lightest colors tend to be dark and will make a room look smaller. Use this to your advantage and choose metallics to create an intimate, dramatic feeling. Emphasize the drama with horizontal stripes, which move your eye around the room, suggesting a kind of ground-hugging coziness, rather than the loftiness verticals can imply. Metallic paints are suitable for any room. Consider a subtle shine for a ceiling or an elegant, stately look for columns.

DECORATIVE TECHNIQUES

4

1 APPLY THE BASE COLOR

Apply the Stonegate metallic base-coat color using the 9-inch metallic roller. Edge along the top, sides, and bottom of the wall in 20-inch sections. Roll on 20-inch-wide strips from top to bottom, using a V motion, until an entire section is covered.

WORK SMARTER

REMEMBER TO SWEEP

It's important to use ceiling-to-floor sweeping motions when applying the base coat color to ensure a uniform finish across the wall.

2 ROLL FROM CEILING TO FLOOR IN ONE MOTION

Without reloading the 9-inch roller, lightly roll from ceiling to floor in one continuous sweep. Avoid overlapping strokes when painting the first coat. Move on to the next 20-inch section repeating Steps 1 and 2 until completed. Allow to dry for four hours. Apply a second coat following the same procedure.

3 MEASURE AND MARK THE STRIPES

Mark off the stripes vertically using a level with printed measurements and a black fine-tip marker. The base color will be dark, so you will need to use a dark marker for readability. (The wall on the opposite page is striped in a pattern of 7-inch, 5-inch, 7-inch, and 10-inch repeating stripes.)

DECORATIVE TECHNIQUES

4

4

MARK GUIDELINES FOR PAINTER'S TAPE

Place marks horizontally every 24 inches or so along the wall as guidelines for low-tack painter's tape.

5

MASK OFF THE STRIPES

Tape off the outside edges of the 5-inch and 10-inch stripes, using 1-inch painter's tape. If desired, use 2-inch tape to ensure that you don't paint over the taped edge. Burnish the edges of the tape with your fingertip for clean lines.

6

APPLY PAINT TO THE WIDEST STRIPE

Apply Turquoise Sea metallic paint to the widest stripes using the 9-inch roller. Without reloading with paint, pull the roller back across the stripe in one continuous motion for an even finish. Allow to dry.

Cool hues of blue and gray metallic paints combine with horizontal stripes to create a dramatic background for contemporary furnishings.

7

APPLY PAINT TO THE NARROWEST STRIPES

Apply Ambassador Sterling metallic paint to the narrowest stripes using the
4½-inch metallic roller and the same technique; allow to dry approximately four
hours. Recoat each color after it has dried.

8

REMOVE TAPE

Remove tape immediately after applying the final coat of paint. Allow the
metallic paint to dry completely.

**The key to the hammered-
metal look is the special roller,
which has a long nap. For a
smoother finish, apply the
paint with a ¼-inch-nap
roller cover.**

Combed stripe

4

DECORATIVE TECHNIQUES

STUFF YOU'LL NEED

BASE COAT: Hazelnut Cream satin finish latex paint

GLAZE COAT: Romantic Isle satin finish latex paint

TOOLS: Drop cloth, paint trays, standard roller frame with 9-inch roller cover (low-nap), 2-inch tapered trim brush, level with printed ruler, blue colored pencil, mini roller frame with 6-inch roller cover, squeegee (12 inches wide), crafts knife, plastic container with printed measurements

MATERIALS: 2-inch low-tack painter's tape, stir sticks, glaze medium, lint-free cotton cloths

TIME TO COMPLETE

Based on a 12×12 foot room, 8 foot ceiling

EXPERIENCED: 8 hrs.

HANDY: 10 hrs.

NOVICE: 12 hrs.

BEFORE YOU BEGIN

Prepare the surface according to pages 40–43. Mask ceiling, baseboards, and trim with painter's tape. Paint the entire wall in the Hazelnut Cream base-coat color. Paint two coats if necessary. Leave tape on; let dry overnight. Notch the blade of a 12-inch-wide squeegee in ⅛-inch sections as shown on page 125. The comb should be wide enough to cover the entire stripe minus 1 inch.

Hazelnut Cream

Romantic Isle

The combed-stripe technique, created by combing overlapping S curves within taped-off stripes, can simulate the look of moiré ribbon or can simply add a lively sense of movement to ordinary stripes. The pattern is created by dragging a notched comb through wet glaze that has been applied over a dry base-coat color. The larger the notches in the comb, the larger the pattern. Prenotched combs are available in various widths at paint centers and art supply stores or you can make a notched comb from a window squeegee as shown on page 125. This finish works best on smooth walls. Practice on a sample board to achieve the desired effect before moving to the wall. Add more glaze or a paint conditioner to the mixture if the glaze dries too quickly. Vertical stripes appear to extend the ceiling, so this finish works well in a small area to add an illusion of height. Try it in a bathroom, entryway, or sunroom. In addition to creating an overlapping S pattern, combing can be used to create straight vertical or horizontal lines, as well as wavy or crosshatched patterns.

1

MEASURE HORIZONTALLY

Measure and mark the stripe widths horizontally every 11 inches using a colored pencil and level with printed ruler. Measure each wall individually. Plan for a solid Hazelnut Cream stripe to fall in each corner rather than a combed stripe. Adjust the measurements as needed to work around doors and windows.

2

DRAW VERTICAL LINES

Extend the measurements vertically with a level and a colored pencil.

 GOOD IDEA

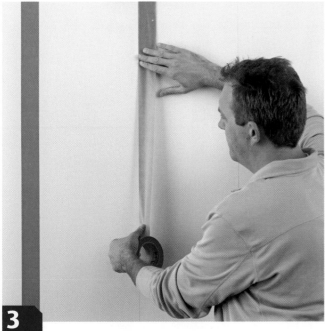

3

MASK OFF ALTERNATING STRIPES

Use low-tack painter's tape to mask off every other stripe. Burnish the edge of the tape with a finger to keep the paint from bleeding underneath the tape.

4

ROLL ON GLAZE

Mix 4 parts glaze to 1 part Romantic Isle latex paint in a plastic container. Use a container with printed measurements for easy measuring. The mixture should roll on easily without running. Adjust the glaze-to-paint ratio if the consistency is too thin. Use a trim brush to cut in the ceiling and trim, then roll glaze onto the first stripe using the 6-inch mini roller. Roll a second time over the entire stripe to ensure a smooth, even finish.

GOOD IDEA

REVIEW YOUR WORK

Step back and look over your work often. This will allow you to go back and reglaze and recomb a stripe before the glaze dries completely.

WORK SMARTER

WORK TOGETHER

If the glaze dries too quickly, have a partner glaze while you comb.

5

DRAG THE SQUEEGEE

Working quickly, start at the top of the wall and drag the squeegee, making a continuous "S" pattern down the wall. Cover the width of the stripe but try not to go outside the edges of the tape.

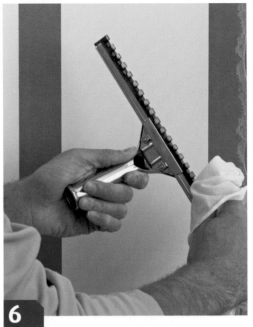

6

KEEP THE SQUEEGEE CLEAN

Wipe excess paint from the squeegee with a cotton cloth.

7

DRAG THE SQUEEGEE IN THE REVERSE DIRECTION

Starting at the top of the wall again, repeat the "S" motion down the wall, but this time reverse the direction.

8

REPEAT THE PROCESS

Remove tape immediately to prevent paint from being pulled off the wall. Repeat the process with every other stripe until the room is completed. Remove all tape and allow the walls to dry overnight.

Don't worry about making perfect S curves and reverse S curves. The technique is fairly forgiving

HORIZONTAL COMBED STRIPES

You can create horizontal as well as vertical stripes. To comb the top stripe, set up a plank and scaffold to walk along. Or restrict the horizontal stripes to the easily reachable area below a chair rail.

Paint combs: Make your own

The comb you use determines the effect you achieve. If you can't find just what you want at your local paint center, make your own using any flexible, waterproof material. Shower squeegees, window-washing squeegees, and plastic bowl scrapers (from the kitchen department of a discount store) are good options. You can even use large-tooth plastic hair combs.

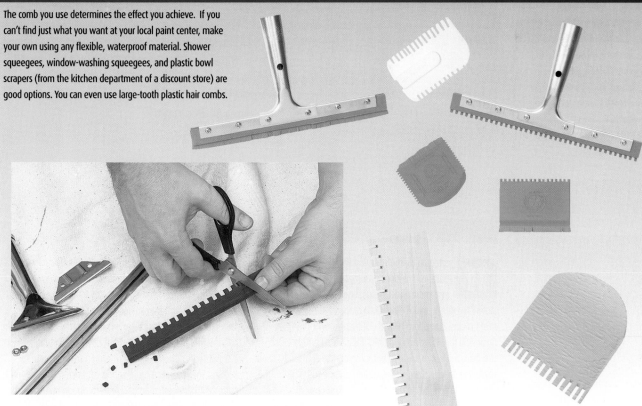

Rubber window-washing squeegees make perfect combs. Mark the teeth with a ruler and marker or utility knife, then cut out with scissors or a crafts knife.

Harlequin diamonds

STUFF YOU'LL NEED

BASE COAT: Timeless Lilac satin finish latex paint

DIAMONDS: Ruffled Iris satin finish latex paint

TOOLS: Drop cloth, paint tray, standard roller frame with 9-inch roller cover, 2-inch tapered trim brush, level with printed ruler, purple colored pencil, mini roller frame with 4-inch roller cover

MATERIALS: 2-inch low-tack painter's tape, stir sticks

TIME TO COMPLETE

Based on a 12×12 foot room, 8 foot ceiling

EXPERIENCED: 16 hrs.

HANDY: 18 hrs.

NOVICE: 20 hrs.

BEFORE YOU BEGIN

Prepare the surface according to pages 40–43. Mask ceiling, baseboards, and trim with painter's tape. Paint the entire wall in the Timeless Lilac base-coat color. Paint two coats if necessary. Leave tape on; let dry overnight.

Timeless Lilac

Ruffled Iris

Harlequin diamonds are a wonderfully versatile pattern. In a child's room, they have a happy energetic effect suggesting the pattern on a clown's costume. In a dining room or living room, a diamond motif is classic and formal without being stuffy. Plan the design so that the diamond height is approximately twice the diamond width. Instead of taping off the diamonds, use a chalk line snapped across the wall to outline the pattern. The chalk line's irregular edges give the design a casual appearance. Another option is to hand-paint the diamonds instead of taping them off. This gives a whimsical look. Complementary colors make a bold statement, while a monochromatic color scheme creates a more sophisticated backdrop. This pattern can easily be combined with other faux-finishing techniques. For a color-washed effect, mix the paint with 4 parts glaze instead of using undiluted paint. Use a crosshatch motion with a trimming brush to create the texture. The result is a more subtle contrast in the diamond pattern. A harlequin diamond pattern needn't be limited to walls. Try this effect on floors and furniture as well.

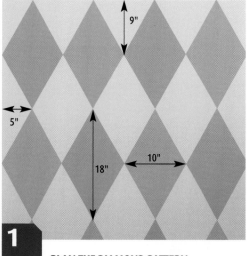

1 PLAN THE DIAMOND PATTERN

Decide on the height and width of the diamond pattern. The diamonds shown are 10 inches wide and 18 inches tall. If you are extending the diamond pattern around the whole room, keep the height of the diamonds the same on every wall, but adjust the width as necessary to fit the wall length. Take the time to work this out on paper. A sketch can help you picture the scale and placement of the diamond pattern so you know where and how to begin marking your measurements.

2 MARK VERTICAL DASHES

Working on one wall at a time, use a level with printed measurements to make vertical dashes every 10 inches. Start on the left-hand side of the wall and move to the right. The first line should start 5 inches from the corner, then every 10 inches after that, ending with a 5-inch measurement on the other side of the wall. Adjust the 10-inch width to match your wall size. For example, if your wall is exactly 10 feet long, then 12 diamonds 10 inches wide will fit perfectly across the wall. If your wall is 9 feet 6 inches long, then you could make the diamonds 9½ inches wide and fit 12 across the wall. Always calculate the width of your wall in inches and divide with the calculator to get a perfect division.

 DESIGN TIP

ADD A DECORATIVE TOUCH
Paint a small dot at each diamond point in a coordinating color or paint a motif on alternating diamonds, such as a simple stenciled flower or leaf, for added interest.

3 DRAW THE VERTICAL LINES

Extend the dashes vertically.

4 MARK THE DIAMOND HEIGHT

Measure and mark the diamond height by making horizontal dashes every 18 inches. The first mark will be 9 inches from the ceiling and every 18 inches after that, ending with 9 inches at the baseboard. Again, adjust the height to fit your walls. Plan for a whole diamond starting at the ceiling and ending at the baseboard. If you prefer, start the pattern at the ceiling and allow it to end at the baseboard where it may.

5
DRAW THE HORIZONTAL LINES

Extend the dashes horizontally across the wall.

6
MARK DIAMOND WIDTH

Each vertical line represents the central axis of a diamond. To mark the side points, measure 5 inches on each side of each vertical line, marking the point on the horizontal lines. Adjust the measurements if the diamonds you are creating are a different size from the 10-inch diamonds shown here.

7
MARK THE TOP AND BOTTOM POINTS

Each horizontal line marks the widest point of the diamond. To mark the top and bottom points of each diamond, measure and mark 9 inches above and below the horizontal line. Adjust the measurement if your diamond height is different from 18 inches.

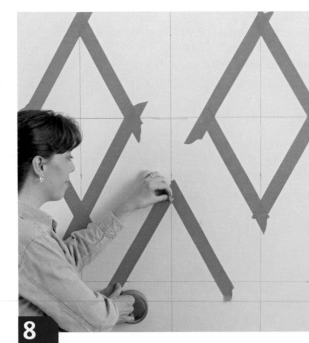

8
MASK OFF ALTERNATING DIAMONDS

Using the points marked in Steps 6 and 7 as your guide, tape off every other diamond. The vertical and horizontal lines will be inside the diamonds, as shown. Press down hard on the painter's tape with a finger.

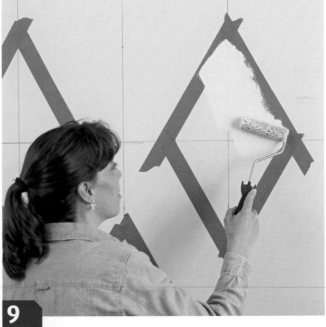

9
REPAINT THE BASE COLOR

Use the 4-inch mini roller and repaint the base-coat color on the taped-off diamonds. This will allow the wall color to bleed underneath the tape instead of the top-coat color. Allow to dry.

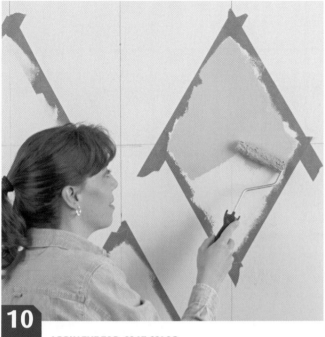

10 APPLY THE TOP-COAT COLOR

Use the 4-inch mini roller and apply the Ruffled Iris latex paint. Apply two coats if necessary. Remove tape and allow to dry.

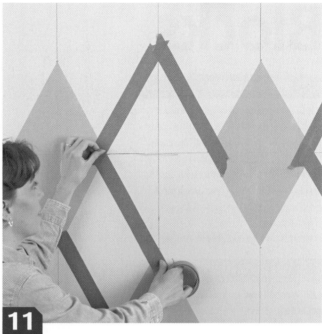

11 MASK OFF REMAINING DIAMONDS

Tape off the remaining diamonds.

A harlequin diamond pattern energizes both formal and informal settings. Flow it around the room or add interest to a focal point wall.

12 REPAINT THE BASE COLOR

Repaint the taped-off diamonds with the Timeless Lilac latex paint.

13 PAINT THE TOP-COAT COLOR

Paint the taped-off diamonds with Ruffled Iris. Recoat if necessary. Remove all remaining tape and allow to dry.

Painting a diamond pattern on your walls demands patience and careful measuring, but the results can be spectacular.

Blocks

4

DECORATIVE TECHNIQUES

✓ STUFF YOU'LL NEED

BASE COAT: Bright Citrus satin finish latex paint
COLOR BLOCKS: Marmalade, Torchlight, Fiery Red,
Fruit Shake, Cheerful Hue satin finish latex paints
TOOLS: Drop cloth, paint tray, standard roller frame
with 9-inch roller cover, 2-inch trim brush, tape
measure, level with printed ruler, colored pencil
(red, orange, or yellow), mini roller frame with
4-inch roller cover
MATERIALS: 2-inch low-tack painter's tape, stir sticks

🕐 TIME TO COMPLETE

Based on a 12×12 foot room, 8 foot ceiling
EXPERIENCED: 16 hrs.
HANDY: 18 hrs.
NOVICE: 20 hrs.

➤ BEFORE YOU BEGIN

Prepare the surface according to pages 40–43. Mask
ceiling, baseboards, and trim with low-tack
painter's tape. Paint the entire wall in the Bright
Citrus base-coat color. Paint two coats if necessary.
Leave tape on and allow to dry overnight.

Bright Citrus

Marmalade

Torchlight

Fiery Red

Fruit Shake

Cheerful Hue

Blocks of color turn boring walls into exciting focal points and can supply character to a room with no architectural features or details. The blocks can be uniform in size and shape, or you can vary the sizes and combine squares and rectangles. The trick is to create a visually balanced arrangement. When planning the design, experiment by arranging painted squares of paper on a table until you like the result. Allow most squares to remain in the base-coat color to minimize the amount of taping and painting. Or eliminate the taping altogether by hand-painting the blocks. For a balanced look, choose colors of the same value or intensity by selecting hues that are in the same position on various paint cards. Colors from the same paint chip produce a sophisticated, monochromatic effect. For a subtle design, choose adjacent colors on the paint chip. Block patterns also work well on the floor. Tape off using the same technique outlined on the pages that follow, or turn the blocks at a 45-degree angle and create a diamond pattern. Finish the floor with matte-finish polyurethane for added durability.

1

MARK THE VERTICAL MEASUREMENTS

The color blocks shown are 22 inches square. Use a tape measure and divide the wall into 22-inch squares. Mark the vertical 22-inch measurements beginning at the ceiling and ending at the floor. If you are blocking the whole room, continue the blocks around the corners, or measure each wall and adjust the block widths to fit. Keep the height of the blocks the same around the room.

2

DRAW THE VERTICAL LINES

Use a level and colored pencil to draw the vertical lines.

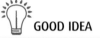

GOOD IDEA

VISUALIZE THE DESIGN
When you are marking, match the pencil color with the block color to help you visualize the design on the wall.

3

MARK THE HORIZONTAL MEASUREMENTS

Mark the horizontal lines with a tape measure.

4

DRAW THE HORIZONTAL LINES

Using a level and colored pencil, draw the horizontal lines, creating squares across the entire wall.

DESIGN TIP

CHANGE THE SCHEME
Try a palette in all cool colors, all tone-on-tone colors, or all neutrals. See pages 23–28 for information about using the color wheel and basic color schemes.

4

DECORATIVE TECHNIQUES

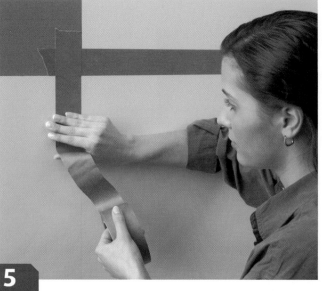

5

MASK OFF

Mask off the squares of one color with low-tack painter's tape. Leave some of the blocks in the original base-coat color. Burnish the edges of the tape with a finger to keep paint from bleeding underneath.

6

REPAINT THE BASE COLOR

Use the mini roller to repaint the Bright Citrus base-coat color onto the block. Allow the base coat to dry.

Blocks are an extremely versatile wall design. Try a pattern in random sizes and colors.

7

PAINT THE FIRST COLOR

Paint all the blocks in the first color. Carefully remove the tape while the paint is still wet so you don't pull up any paint.

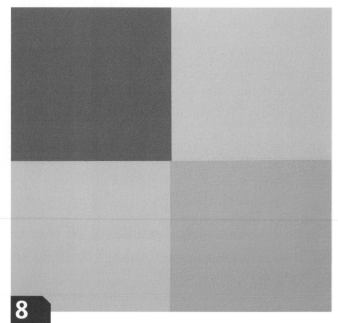

8

REPEAT THE PROCESS

Repeat the taping and painting process with all other colors, painting one color at a time, allowing the blocks to dry in between.

Allover stenciling

STUFF YOU'LL NEED

BASE COAT: Aged Mint satin finish latex paint

STENCIL COAT: Capri and Big Sur Blue satin finish latex paints

TOOLS: Drop cloth, paint tray, standard roller frame with 9-inch roller cover, 2-inch tapered trim brush, level with printed ruler, graphite or green colored pencil, stencil brush (medium size)

MATERIALS: 2-inch low-tack painter's tape, stir sticks, Florentine Damask Medium stencil, stencil spray adhesive, paper towels

TIME TO COMPLETE

Based on a 12×12 foot room, 8 foot ceiling

EXPERIENCED: 16 hrs.

HANDY: 20 hrs.

NOVICE: 24 hrs.

BEFORE YOU BEGIN

Prepare the surface according to pages 40–43. Mask the ceiling, baseboards, and trim with low-tack painter's tape. Paint the entire wall in the Aged Mint base-coat color. Paint two coats if necessary. Leave tape on and allow to dry overnight.

Aged Mint

Capri

Big Sur Blue

Stenciling is one of the oldest techniques for decorating walls. Before the mid-1800s, stenciling was actually less expensive than wallpaper. Now, even though wallpaper is economical, there are still good reasons to opt for an allover stencil pattern: You have complete control over color choice, you can create your own unique design, and you can customize the look to suit your style. A precut stencil was used for the room above (see page 187). The key to the design is to properly line up the pattern by establishing vertical and horizontal lines. Use a level with printed ruler or a laser level for easy measuring. When stenciling, avoid overloading the brush with paint. Too much paint causes bleeding underneath the stencil and results in a heavy-looking finish. Instead, blot the brush onto a paper towel, and then pounce or stipple the paint into the stencil cutout using a circular motion. A cloudy, translucent appearance is the desired effect. As an option to stenciling an allover pattern, try a border along the ceiling, at chair-rail height, or along the baseboard.

4

1

DRAW A STRAIGHT VERTICAL LINE
For a perfectly aligned stencil pattern, establish a straight vertical line in the middle of your wall with the level. Draw a light line from ceiling to floor using a graphite pencil or a green colored pencil.

2

POSITION THE FIRST STENCIL
This stencil is actually one-quarter of the pattern. The repeating pattern is made by stenciling the single repeat in four different positions, creating mirror images. Spray the stencil with adhesive and position it on the wall, lining up the registration marks on the stencil with the vertical line drawn in Step 1. Begin stenciling by dipping a medium-size stencil brush into the Capri latex paint, then blotting most of the paint onto a paper towel. Stipple the brush over the stencil, pouncing in several layers to add more color. Use a circular motion to give the image dimension. In this step, the Capri paint is not stenciled solid, but lighter in some areas and darker in others. With a separate stencil brush, stipple a little Big Sur Blue paint into the stencil for shadows.

3

DRAW THE REGISTRATION MARKS ONTO THE WALL
Use a pencil to make registration marks on the wall, or simply stencil the marks onto the wall. Penciled registration marks can be erased later.

Stenciling calls for the merest whisper of paint. Swirl the brush onto a paper towel before applying it to the stencil.

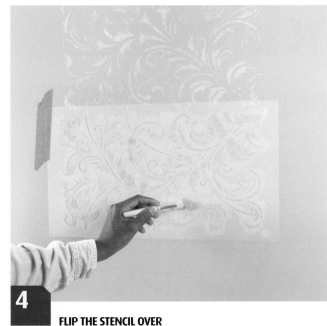

4 FLIP THE STENCIL OVER

Remove the stencil and flip it over, lining it up below the previously stenciled area. (If you can rub any paint off the stencil with your finger, clean it first with denatured alcohol. The paint should, however, dry almost instantly.) Use the previous registration marks as your guide for aligning the stencil with the vertical line. Stipple Capri latex paint through the stencil, avoiding solid coverage. With a medium-size brush, add a small amount of Big Sur Blue latex paint as an accent. Repeat until the first vertical row is complete, flipping the stencil as you go.

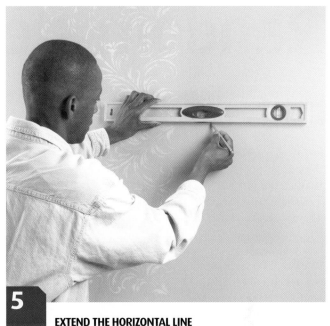

5 EXTEND THE HORIZONTAL LINE

Draw a horizontal line, lining up with one set of registration marks, to establish the placement of the horizontal line on the wall. Extend this line all the way across your wall.

6 STENCIL ONE HORIZONTAL ROW

Stencil one horizontal row, using the horizontal level line and the previous registration marks as your guide. Refer to the picture that comes with the pattern to ensure correct positioning of the repeat. Apply the Capri and Big Sur Blue paints as in Step 4. Repeat Steps 2–6 to cover the wall on both sides of the vertical line marked in Step 1. Remove any remaining tape and allow to dry.

Stenciling an entire wall is ambitious but creative and allows you to create a look that is uniquely your own. When you finish the job, clean the stencil immediately by soaking it in hot water for a few minutes. Remove paint from stubborn areas by rubbing gently with a finger. Store the stencil either flat or rolled up.

Random stenciling

DECORATIVE TECHNIQUES

4

✓ STUFF YOU'LL NEED

BASE COAT: Spruce Tint satin finish latex paint

TOP COAT: Bird's Nest satin finish latex paint

TOOLS: Drop cloth, paint tray, standard roller frame with 9-inch roller cover, 2-inch tapered trim brush, stenciling brush, small artist's brush, scissors, pencil

MATERIALS: 2-inch low-tack painter's tape, stir sticks, Cherry Blossom stencil, roll of 24-inch tracing paper, stencil spray adhesive, scrap board, lint-free cotton cloths or paper towels

🕐 TIME TO COMPLETE

Based on a 12×12 foot room, 8 foot ceiling

EXPERIENCED: 5 hrs.

HANDY: 6.5 hrs.

NOVICE: 8.5 hrs.

🖐 BEFORE YOU BEGIN

Prepare the surface according to pages 40–43. Mask ceiling, baseboards, and trim with painter's tape. Paint the entire wall in the Spruce Tint base-coat color. Paint two coats if necessary. Leave tape on; let dry overnight.

Spruce Tint

Bird's Nest

🖌 TOOL SAVVY

SPRAY IT ON
Tape the stencil to the wall or spray the back with a stencil spray adhesive. The adhesive is long-lasting and won't leave residue.

A s the name suggests, random stenciling involves applying stencil designs to portions of the wall to suggest a hand-painted design. This cherry blossom stencil consists of a sheet of component parts that you can arrange and combine to create designs that mimic the natural growth of cherry tree branches (see page 187). Working on tracing paper, practice assembling the various parts of the stencil to build a design that works in your room. This drawing will guide you when you move to the wall, but you'll still have creative freedom to change the position of the stencils since there are no guidelines drawn on the wall. To emphasize the hand-painted effect, try applying the paint more lightly at the edges of the stencil for a faded effect or vary the tones of the blossoms and leaves to create interest. When shading, always start with the lightest color and finish with the darkest. Mistakes can simply be painted out and re-stenciled. This design works for both walls and floors, as well as furniture, such as cabinet panels.

1 TRACE SECTIONS OF THE STENCIL
The stencil will come in multiple segments on a sheet. Cut the stencil apart. Tape a 3-foot piece of tracing paper along the edge of the ceiling. With a pencil, trace sections of the stencil to get a feel for how the different pattern parts work together. Begin with the larger branches coming from the ceiling or from behind a window and alternate blossoms and branches using smaller branch sections as the limb extends. Overlap the branch sections with the blossoms and leaves as you go.

2

FILL IN THE STENCIL

When you are comfortable building the design, take down the tracing paper and use it for reference as you begin to stencil. Dip the stencil brush into a small amount of Bird's Nest latex paint and tap out onto a scrap board until the paint is evenly distributed on the bristle ends. For lighter areas or fading, wipe the brush first onto a paper towel or cotton cloth. Hold the stencil section in position or spray the back with adhesive and use a light circular tapping motion to fill in the stencil. Allow each application to dry slightly before adding to it. Once you have a number of branches started, you can move around while you are waiting for areas to dry.

3

FADE THE PATTERN AT THE END OF EACH BRANCH

When you approach the end of the branch, trace only part of the blossom or leaves, tapering off or fading the patterns. Isolate a blossom on one of the stencil parts by taping off the surrounding leaves. Scatter a couple of falling blossoms down the wall and repeat with a couple of small leaves, as if they are falling to the floor. Continue this process until completed.

4

DECORATIVE TECHNIQUES

4

DEFINE AREAS THAT OVERLAP

Use the Spruce Tint base color and a small artist's liner brush and define the areas where the patterns overlapped. For example, retrace the edge of a leaf or petal that has overlapped a branch. This will keep the design from looking flat or muddy. Remove tape and allow to dry.

Stenciling brings out your inner artist. This technique goes beyond the purely functional need to protect wall surfaces and gives you the chance to express yourself creatively.

Versatile design

By reversing or flipping the stencil, you can suggest branches growing up from the floor.

Embossed stenciling

✓ STUFF YOU'LL NEED

BASE COAT: Overcast flat finish latex paint

GLAZE COAT: Manuscript flat finish latex paint

TOOLS: Drop cloth, paint tray, standard roller frame with 9-inch roller cover, 2-inch tapered trim brush, mini roller with 6-inch roller cover, 4-inch plastic trowel, level with printed ruler, pencil

MATERIALS: Arabian Border stencil, Far Eastern Flower stencil (custom-cut for compatibility with border), 2-inch low-tack painter's tape, stir sticks, joint compound, glaze medium, 100-grit sandpaper, lint-free cotton cloths

🕐 TIME TO COMPLETE

Based on a 12×12 foot room, 8 foot ceiling

EXPERIENCED: 10 hrs.

HANDY: 12.5 hrs.

NOVICE: 15.5 hrs.

↻ BEFORE YOU BEGIN

Prepare the surface according to pages 40–43. Mask ceiling, baseboards, and trim with painter's tape. Paint the entire wall in the Overcast base-coat color. Paint two coats if necessary. Leave tape on; allow to dry overnight.

Overcast

Manuscript

A dd an elegant embossed design to the wall with dimensional stenciling. Also called relief stenciling, this effect is created by applying joint compound to a stencil pattern using a trowel or blade. (You could also use Venetian plaster.) After the joint compound is dry, the base color is applied to the design and sanded. A thin layer of glaze is rolled on and ragged off to add more depth to the finish. Do not apply the base color too heavily over the embossed stencil or it will be difficult to sand

through and reveal the pattern. For a dramatic appearance, use a deep base color, such as red, and a rich pure glaze such as gold. Stencils designed for this technique are made from heavy plastic. When ordering, request that the stencils be cut for embossing (see page 187). A corner stencil and border stencil were combined to create the panels above. This finish is also effective on other hard surfaces, such as square columns, fireplace surrounds, mirrors, and cabinet doors.

1
MARK THE BORDER GUIDELINES

Lay out borders on the wall by marking guidelines for the outer edges only. Use a level to ensure that your lines are straight.

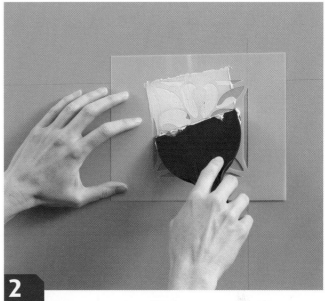

2
POSITION THE CORNER STENCIL

Begin by positioning the flower motif in a corner and apply joint compound with a 4-inch plastic trowel. Lift the stencil off and repeat for each corner. Rinse the stencil occasionally to prevent the pattern from filling as the joint compound dries. Use spray adhesive on the back of the stencil to help hold the stencil in place if desired, or tack it in place with blue painter's tape.

3
MARK OFF THE BORDER STENCIL

Mark off the repeat of the border stencil using the holes provided in the pattern. It is only necessary to mark along one side.

4
APPLY JOINT COMPOUND TO THE BORDER STENCIL

Using the same technique as for the corner motifs, apply the border stencil. Stencil alternating border sections and allow them to dry.

5 STENCIL REMAINING AREAS

After the first set has dried a couple of hours, fill in the remaining sections. When you are working next to a corner motif, apply joint compound just up to the edge. Use the end of the trowel to make a sharp edge. Allow to dry overnight.

6 APPLY BASE COLOR OVER EMBOSSED AREAS

Use a mini roller to apply a light coat of the base color over the embossed motif. Allow to dry approximately two hours.

7 SAND TO REVEAL PATTERN

Sand the motif firmly until most of the pattern is revealed.

8 REMOVE DUST

Wipe off sanding dust with a cotton cloth.

4

DECORATIVE TECHNIQUES

9 **ROLL ON GLAZE**
Make a thin glaze mixture of 1 part Manuscript to 7 parts glaze medium in a container. Apply to one small 2-foot section at a time.

10 **WIPE OFF GLAZE**
Use a lint-free cotton cloth to lightly lift off the glaze. This will lightly tint the walls and create a soft, faded look, as well as seal the exposed joint compound.

Dimensional stenciling gives flat, ordinary surfaces a distinctive, sophisticated look. Try this technique on columns or furniture, too.

 11 **ALLOW TO DRY**
Remove all remaining tape and allow glaze to dry.

Denim

4

DECORATIVE TECHNIQUES

✓ STUFF YOU'LL NEED

BASE COAT: Cowgirl Blue semigloss finish latex paint
GLAZE COAT: Blue Print
TOOLS: Drop cloth, paint tray, standard roller frame with 9-inch roller cover, 2-inch tapered trim brush, tape measure, level with printed ruler, blue colored pencil, 7-inch denim weaver brush, 4-inch denim check roller
MATERIALS: 2-inch low-tack painter's tape, stir sticks, lint-free cotton cloths

🕐 TIME TO COMPLETE

Based on a 12×12 foot room, 8 foot ceiling
EXPERIENCED: 10 hrs.
HANDY: 12 hrs.
NOVICE: 14 hrs.

🡆 BEFORE YOU BEGIN

Prepare the surface according to pages 40–43. Mask ceiling, baseboards, and trim with low-tack painter's tape. Paint the wall in the Cowgirl Blue base-coat color. Paint two coats if necessary. Leave the tape on and allow to dry overnight.

Cowgirl Blue

Blue Print

The denim wall finish mimics the casual, worn texture of the popular fabric. The technique requires a tinted glaze mixture and two faux-finishing tools—a denim weaver brush and a denim check roller. It's a good technique to try if you're a beginner because it's hard to mess up—if you don't like the effect, just brush it out and reapply the glaze. Sectioning the walls into a series of narrow, vertical panels allows one person to complete each step quickly. The painting experts at The Home Depot recommend that you remove the painter's tape while the paint is still wet; let the paint dry for 24 hours, then tape off the remaining sections. This finish works best on smooth walls. To play up the denim look, emphasize the "seams" (see "Design Tip," page 143) with broken white lines to simulate stitches. Or glue real denim pockets to the wall and tuck in snapshots or postcards for fun wall art. This technique also looks good in colors other than the standard denim blue, such as red or green.

1 **DIVIDE THE ROOM**
Divide the room into a series of vertical panels. Keep the width of the panels between 18 and 36 inches so you can work quickly from top to bottom. Horizontal panels are also appropriate for this technique. Measure horizontally for the panel widths using a tape measure.

 **WORK SMARTER**

PICK YOUR PENCIL
Use a colored pencil or watercolor pencil rather than a graphite pencil so your marks do not show through the glaze.

2 **DRAW VERTICAL LINES**
Use a level along with a colored pencil that matches the paint color to draw vertical lines that complete the panels.

DESIGN TIP

CREATE A SEAM
Give denim walls a realistic appearance by adding "seams." Overlapping panel edges slightly creates dark vertical lines or seams. For seams, place the tape on top of the dried glaze approximately ⅛ inch from the edge. When the next section is painted, this area will receive a double layer of glaze and will be darker.

3 **MASK EVERY OTHER PANEL**
Mask off alternating panels with low-tack painter's tape. Treat sections that meet in a corner as two alternating panels.

BUYER'S GUIDE

DON'T BUY TOO MUCH
One gallon of glaze and one quart of paint are usually enough to cover a 25×20-foot room.

WORK SMARTER

THE RIGHT MIX
The glaze used here is a premixed glaze, but you can mix your own by buying semigloss paint in the color of your choice and a gallon of untinted glaze medium. See page 35 for guidelines on glaze mixtures.

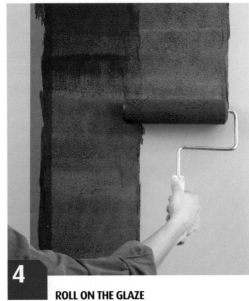

4
ROLL ON THE GLAZE
Roll the Blue Print glaze onto the first masked-off panel. Use a trim brush to fill in tight corners and other hard-to-reach areas.

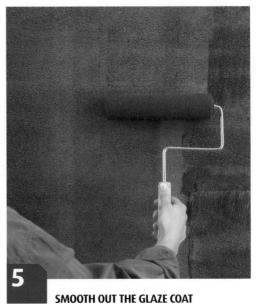

5
SMOOTH OUT THE GLAZE COAT
Immediately roll through the glaze a second time, using long floor-to-ceiling strokes to make certain the coat is smooth and consistent.

6
DRAG WITH A WEAVER BRUSH
Drag the denim weaver brush through the glaze with horizontal strokes. Start and stop on the taped line to prevent the glaze from building up. When working in a corner, drag in one direction from the corner outward.

7
KEEP THE BRUSH CLEAN
Wipe the brush with a damp, lint-free cloth after each stroke to remove excess glaze.

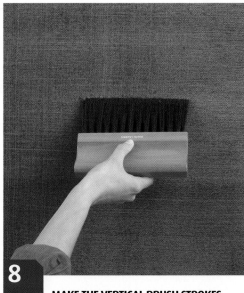

WORK SMARTER

GET SOME HELP
Try working with a partner. One person could roll on the glaze, and the other person could apply the texture. The process would go faster and be more fun.

8
MAKE THE VERTICAL BRUSH STROKES
Drag the brush through the glaze using vertical strokes. Wipe with a damp, lint-free cloth after each stroke.

9
APPLY CHECK ROLLER
Using firm pressure, run the denim check roller horizontally over the newly brushed section.

10
FINISH THE CHECK PATTERN
Run the denim check roller vertically through the same section. Create as much pattern as you desire. Wipe often with a damp, lint-free cloth to remove excess glaze. Complete the entire panel. Remove tape.

11
REPEAT THE PROCESS
Move on to the next panel, mask it off with the low-tack painter's tape, and repeat Steps 4–10. Repeat the steps for the remaining panels. When finished, remove all tape; allow to dry.

4

DECORATIVE TECHNIQUES

Stripe-and-Stencil combination

✓ STUFF YOU'LL NEED

BASE COAT: Coastal Mist satin finish latex paint

STRIPE & STENCIL COATS: Hushed White semigloss latex paint

STENCIL COATS: Primrose Garden, Fresh Heather, Fresh Peaches, Mango Madness, and Peas in a Pod satin finish latex paints

TOOLS: Drop cloth, paint tray, standard roller frame with 9-inch roller cover, 2-inch tapered trim brush, level with printed ruler, mini roller frame with 4-inch roller cover, scissors, crafts knife, six medium-sized stencil brushes

MATERIALS: 1½-inch low-tack painter's tape, stir sticks, poster board or self-healing cutting mat, paint pens in Petal Pink, Lilac, and White satin finishes, white colored pencil, stencil spray adhesive, stencil patterns (see pages 182–184), paper towels, disposable plate, lint-free cotton cloth

🕐 TIME TO COMPLETE

Based on a 12×12 foot room, 8 foot ceiling
EXPERIENCED: 6 hrs.
HANDY: 8 hrs.
NOVICE: 10 hrs.

🐦 BEFORE YOU BEGIN

Prepare the surface according to pages 40–43. Mask ceiling, baseboards, and trim with low-tack painter's tape. Paint the wall in the Coastal Mist base-coat color. Paint two coats if necessary. Remove tape and allow to dry overnight. Make copies of the flower patterns provided on pages 182–184. Use a photocopier to enlarge the pattern to the desired size. The enlargement suggestions printed with the flower patterns produce the results shown. Fit as many as you can on one sheet, leaving a 1- or 2-inch border around each flower so you can cut them apart later. Have the patterns soft laminated at a copy shop and make several copies of each pattern.

Two popular decorative paint finishes combine in this charming bedroom.

A painted white stripe at plate-rail height anchors an array of stenciled flowers. The stencils were custom-made. (You'll find patterns on pages 182–184.) Always stencil the flower outline first, then fill in the center. Coordinating or contrasting paint pen colors give the flowers additional details. Dots, dashes, or just basic outlining are a few ways to accentuate the flowers using paint pens. The flowers can be positioned randomly in relationship to the stripe. Place some flowers on the stripe and allow others to fall below it, as shown above, or line them up above and below the stripe if you prefer a more orderly

arrangement. This design could easily be changed to accommodate a boy's room by using the same stripe-and-stencil combination, but using a sports theme for the stencils. Make stencil designs for baseballs, basketballs, and footballs and use a palette of red, blue, taupe, and cream.

To create your own stencil designs, study a ready-made pattern to see how the outline is cut for various effects. If you find inspiration in printed material, make sure the artwork is not copyrighted and is free for use. Have a copy shop enlarge the pattern to the desired size and copy it to transparency film. Cut out the pattern carefully with a crafts knife, working on a piece of poster board or self-healing cutting mat.

Coastal Mist	Hushed White	Primrose Garden

Fresh Heather	Fresh Peaches	Mango Madness	Peas in a Pod

1

MEASURE THE STRIPE

Measure for a 4-inch stripe to run horizontally across the walls by measuring up from the floor 6 feet or the desired height and making two horizontal dashes 4 inches apart.

2

DRAW THE HORIZONTAL LINES

Extend these lines horizontally with a level and a white colored pencil.

3

MASK OFF THE LINES

Tape off the lines with low-tack painter's tape, pressing down hard with your fingertips to prevent paint from bleeding underneath.

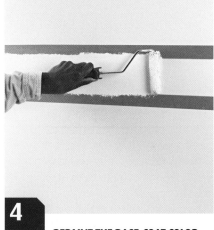

4

REPAINT THE BASE-COAT COLOR

Repaint the stripe with the Coastal Mist latex paint. This helps seal the tape edges, and if paint seeps under the tape, it will be the base-coat color and will blend with the rest of the wall. Allow to dry.

5

APPLY WHITE PAINT

Apply the Hushed White paint onto the stripe with the 4-inch mini roller, trimming in where appropriate. Apply two coats if necessary. Remove tape while paint is still wet. Allow to dry.

6

CUT AROUND THE FLOWER EDGES

Cut apart the stencils using scissors. Leave a 1-inch border around each flower. Cut around the flower edges (shown in purple for overlay 1) using a crafts knife. Use a safe cutting surface such as a poster board or self-healing cutting mat. Using another copy of the flower, cut out the flower center (shown in pink, overlay 2), leaving a border 1 inch wide or more. (See page 182 for details.)

7

STENCIL THE FLOWER PETALS

Spray stencil adhesive on the back of the stencil or use small pieces of painter's tape to adhere the stencil to the wall. Stencil the main part of the largest flower in Primrose Garden latex paint. Dip the stencil brush into the paint, blotting excess onto a paper towel. Begin stenciling by using a pouncing motion, with the brush almost perpendicular to the wall. Stencil several thin coats instead of one thick coat to prevent the paint from bleeding underneath. Wipe the stencil occasionally with a lint-free cloth to remove paint buildup. Let dry.

8

STENCIL THE FLOWER CENTER

Stencil the flower center in the same manner with Fresh Heather latex paint. Allow to dry before adding details with the paint pens.

9

OUTLINE THE FLOWER PETALS

Outline the flower using the Petal Pink paint pen.

10

OUTLINE THE FLOWER CENTER

Use the Petal Pink paint pen to outline the flower center with broken lines.

4

DECORATIVE TECHNIQUES

11

ADD LINEAR DETAILS
Add details to the flower petals using the White paint pen.

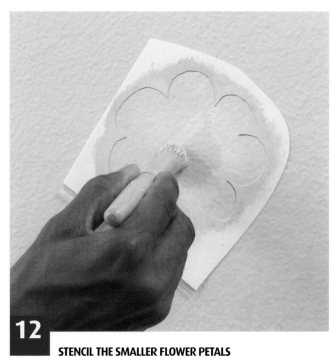

12

STENCIL THE SMALLER FLOWER PETALS
Use the same process to stencil the smaller flower with the Fresh Heather latex paint.

13

STENCIL THE FLOWER CENTER
Stencil the white center of the flower in the same manner using the Hushed White latex paint.

14

OUTLINE THE FLOWER
Add details to the flower with the Lilac paint pen.

15
STENCIL THE FLOWER PETALS
Use the same process to stencil another smaller flower with Fresh Heather paint.

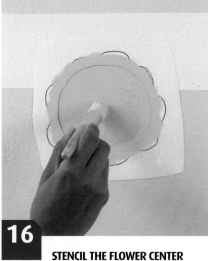

16
STENCIL THE FLOWER CENTER
Stencil the large green center in the same manner using the Peas in a Pod latex paint.

17
OUTLINE THE CENTER
Outline the flower center with the White paint pen.

18
OUTLINE THE PETALS
Outline the flower petals using the Petal Pink paint pen.

19
ALLOW TO DRY
Continue stenciling flowers and adding details with the paint pens until completed. Remove any remaining tape. Allow flowers to dry. Clean stencils so they are ready for the next use: Immerse in hot water and allow them to soak for a few minutes. Remove paint by rubbing gently with a finger. Store stencils either flat or rolled up.

 DESIGN TIP

STENCIL ACCESSORIES TO MATCH
Use one or more of the flower patterns to stencil a pot or bulletin board to match the room design.

4

DECORATIVE TECHNIQUES

Clouds

STUFF YOU'LL NEED

BASE COAT: Seasport satin finish latex paint
CLOUDS: Water Lily and Coastal Blue satin finish latex paints
TOOLS: Drop cloth, paint tray, standard roller frame with 9-inch roller cover, 2-inch tapered trim brush, two plastic containers with lids
MATERIALS: 2-inch low-tack painter's tape, stir sticks, cloud kit, glaze medium, water

TIME TO COMPLETE

Based on a 12×12 foot room, 8 foot ceiling
EXPERIENCED: 12 hrs.
HANDY: 14 hrs.
NOVICE: 16 hrs.

BEFORE YOU BEGIN

Prepare the surface according to pages 40–43. Mask ceiling, baseboards, and trim with low-tack painter's tape. Paint the entire wall in the Seasport base-coat color. Paint two coats if necessary. Leave tape on; allow to dry overnight.

Seasport

Water Lily

Coastal Blue

4

DECORATIVE TECHNIQUES

Clouds painted over a blue sky add a tranquil, peaceful feeling to any child's room. The wall shown was created using a kit packed with all the tools necessary to paint billowy clouds over a graduated background (see page 187). The kit includes a large and small natural sheepskin pad, a large brush, two small brushes, and a paint tray with three compartments. The large natural sheepskin pad picks up two to six paint colors at one time, blending them to create a three-dimensional look. Start the effect by painting the background colors so that the sky seems lighter at the horizon and becomes deeper and purer as your eye moves up. Across the background, paint a variety of shapely clouds that appear level on the bottom and puffy at the top. Vary the sizes and the placement of the clouds, wrapping some around the corners. A cloud motif fits perfectly into a child's bedroom, playroom, nursery, or bath. Clouds can also be painted above a chair rail offset by a pattern of stripes or checks.

TOOL SAVVY

TAKE CARE OF YOUR TOOL
Before using the natural sheepskin tool, remove lint with masking tape. When you are finished painting, simply wash the tool with warm water (do not use soap) and blot with a towel to dry. Remove any dried paint with a wire painter's brush.

1

APPLY A STREAK OF WHITE GLAZE

Mix 1 part Water Lily paint, 1 part water, and 2 parts glaze in a plastic container. Use a container with printed measurements for easy measuring. In a second plastic container, mix 1 part Coastal Blue paint, 1 part water, and 2 parts glaze. Set the Coastal Blue glaze aside. With the white glaze mixture and the large brush from the cloud kit, apply one streak of Water Lily glaze just above the baseboard.

2

TAP OUT THE GLAZE WITH THE PAD

Use the large sheepskin pad to tap out the glaze, making it fade into the blue base-coat color. Make the lower 2 feet of the wall the lightest part, so it resembles the horizon. Continue brushing on white glaze and tapping it out, blending it into the blue base coat as you work around the room. Do not try to make a straight line anywhere, but rather tap the glaze out to allow it to fade away. Continue until the entire lower portion of the room is complete. Do not stop in the middle of a wall, but instead, keep working with wet edges until the wall is completed.

3

APPLY DARK BLUE GLAZE

Using the darker Coastal Blue glaze, apply one brush stroke of glaze, but this time closer to the ceiling line.

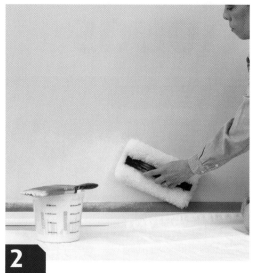

4

TAP OUT THE GLAZE WITH THE PAD

Tap out the glaze with the large sheepskin pad, allowing it to fade into the lighter blue base-coat color moving downward. Aim for about 2 feet until the darker blue fades away with lines that are not crisp. Continue until the entire room or wall is completed. Allow to dry.

DESIGN TIP

ONE OR TWO
Single-color clouds are usually created using a white glaze. Create two-color clouds using white and gray glazes.

5 **BRUSH ON WHITE GLAZE IN AN ARCH**
To make the clouds, use the white glaze and the smaller brush, and paint an arch of white where you want a cloud to appear.

6 **TAP OUT THE GLAZE TO FORM CLOUDS**
Immediately begin tapping out the top edge of the glaze arch with the mini brush, creating an uneven edge. Blend the bottom of the cloud until white glaze fades away, blending into the blue background.

7 **REPEAT FOR ADDITIONAL CLOUDS**
Continue adding more clouds using Steps 5–6. Overlap the clouds as desired.

8 **ADD CLOUD WISPS**
Using the same process as for the larger clouds, paint small clouds between the groups of larger ones. Use the white glaze and the smaller brush, and paint an arch of white where you want a smaller cloud to appear.

9 **TAP OUT THE GLAZE TO FORM SMALL BITS OF CLOUDS**
Immediately begin tapping out the top edge of the glaze arch with the mini brush, creating an uneven edge to your cloud. When clouds are completed, remove remaining tape and allow to dry.

Chalkboard paint

✓ STUFF YOU'LL NEED

PRIMER: Deep Base Primer tinted to match Hunting Coat Red
BASE COAT: Hunting Coat Red semigloss finish latex paint
TOOLS: Drop cloth, tack cloth, 2½-inch tapered trim brush
MATERIALS: Chalkboard paint, painted or unfinished furniture, 120-grit sandpaper, stir sticks, 2-inch low-tack painter's tape

🕐 TIME TO COMPLETE

Based on the cabinets as shown
EXPERIENCED: 8 hrs.
HANDY: 9 hrs.
NOVICE: 10 hrs.

↻ BEFORE YOU BEGIN

Prepare the unfinished wood cabinets by sanding lightly with 120-grit sandpaper and wiping with a tack cloth. Remove the doors and hinges from the cabinets, or tape off the hinges with low-tack painter's tape to protect from paint.

Hunting Coat Red

📖 WORK SMARTER

TINT YOUR PRIMER
Most primers can be tinted to ensure ample coverage when you apply the finish coat. Too much paint will dilute the primer and reduce its efficiency. It's a good idea to follow the manufacturer's recommendations.

Chalkboard paint can turn any wall, table, door, counter, or cabinet into a writable and erasable chalkboard. The paint is easy to apply to any smooth surface using a trim brush or mini roller. If used, low-tack painter's tape should be removed immediately while the paint is still wet. Follow the manufacturer's instructions to season the finish by rubbing it with chalk. One quart of chalkboard paint will go a long way. The paint can also be applied to metal, plastic, wood, or glass surfaces. Try it in a game room, playroom, family room, or child's bedroom.

1

PRIME THE CABINET

Prime the entire cabinet with the Hunting Coat Red tinted primer. Allow to dry.

2

BASE COAT WITH LATEX

Apply the base coat of Hunting Coat Red latex paint. Do not paint the inner panels of the outer doors. Allow to dry 36 hours, then apply a second coat if necessary. Allow to dry.

Chalkboards can be used all over the house as message boards or for creative play.

Preparing furniture

1

SAND TO BARE WOOD

Whether the piece is finished or unfinished, sand it to bare wood with at least 120-grit sandpaper. Fill dings, dents, and holes with wood filler.

2

PRIME THE SURFACE

Spot prime knots, pitch pockets, or other discoloration. Then prime the entire surface.

WORK SMARTER

MANY USES FOR CHALKBOARD PAINT

You can also use chalkboard paint on the wall inside a painted border, on a child's tabletop, or over a cork bulletin board.

3

PAINT THE INNER PANELS

Tape off the door panels with low-tack painter's tape. Paint the panels with chalkboard paint. Allow to dry, then recoat if necessary. Remove tape and allow to dry.

4

ADD A DISTRESSED LOOK

Sand the edges of the cabinet doors and cabinet body to add a distressed look. Use 120-grit sandpaper alone or on a sanding block.

5

ATTACH THE CABINETS TO THE WALL

To hang, attach cabinets to wall studs, following all manufacturer's instructions.

Wicker

✓ STUFF YOU'LL NEED

BASE COAT: Costa Mesa semigloss finish latex paint

GLAZE COAT: Golden Oak gel stain

TOOLS: Drop cloth, 2-inch tapered trim brush, ruler, pencil, shower squeegee, small utility knife, 2-inch chip brush

MATERIALS: Primer, 150-grit sandpaper, lint-free cotton cloths, 2-inch low-tack painter's tape, 1-inch low-tack painter's tape, stir sticks, scrap foam core or cardboard

🕐 TIME TO COMPLETE

Based on 3×4-foot dresser

EXPERIENCED: 5 hrs.

HANDY: 6 hrs.

NOVICE: 7 hrs.

Costa Mesa

Golden Oak

Transform a secondhand unfinished piece of furniture with the woven look of faux-wicker. This trendy look is perfect for garden rooms, bedrooms, or casual living spaces. The key to creating the look is to use a notched squeegee; you can easily make your own tool by cutting notches in the rubber blade of a shower squeegee. It's a good idea to practice the technique on a piece of scrap board until you are comfortable with the procedure of dragging and lifting the squeegee to create the woven texture. The effect works best on flat surfaces such as an armoire, tabletop, door, or even on the wall below a chair rail. For a warm, natural wicker look, choose hues of tan and gold. For a bolder effect try brick red or sage green.

4

DECORATIVE TECHNIQUES

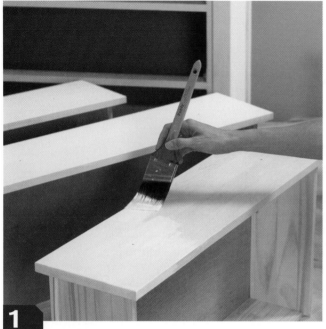

1

PRIME THE PIECE
Prime the piece using a 2-inch tapered trim brush.

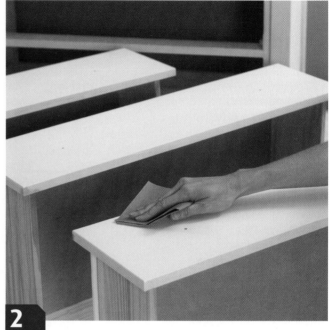

2

SAND LIGHTLY
If your piece has not previously been painted, the wood grain will rise slightly after priming. Lightly sand the surface with 150-grit sandpaper.

3

REMOVE EXCESS DUST
Wipe off excess dust with a clean cotton rag.

4

APPLY THE BASE COAT
Using a 2-inch tapered trim brush, paint your piece with Costa Mesa latex. Apply two coats. Allow the first coat to dry before applying the second.

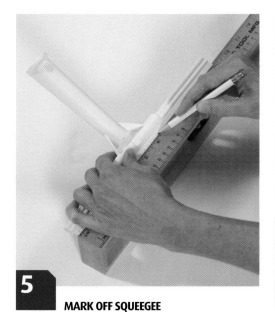

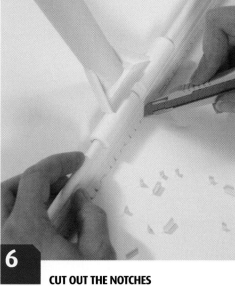

WORK SMARTER

MOVE QUICKLY
You will need to drag the squeegee quickly across the surface once the gel stain has been applied.

5 MARK OFF SQUEEGEE

Lay the edge of the squeegee along the edge of a ruler and mark off notches with a pencil, alternating five ⅛-inch notches with one ⅜-inch notch.

6 CUT OUT THE NOTCHES

Place the squeegee blade flat onto a cutting surface, such as foam core. Use a small utility knife to cut out the ⅜-inch notches and every other ⅛-inch notch. The resulting edge of the blade will have three ⅛-inch "teeth" separated by a ⅜-inch gap repeating across the edge.

4

DECORATIVE TECHNIQUES

7 MASK OFF SIDES AND DRAWER FRONTS

Tape off the side panels and drawer fronts. Use 2-inch low-tack painter's tape on the side panels and 1-inch tape on the drawer fronts. Burnish the edge of the tape with a fingernail to ensure a clean, finished edge when it is removed.

8 BRUSH ON STAIN

Brush on Golden Oak gel stain with a 2-inch chip brush. Cover the entire panel. Brush with the grain of the wood. Work on only one panel at a time.

9

PULL THE SQUEEGEE VERTICALLY

Drag the squeegee vertically through the stain, using the edge of the tape as your guide. Use both hands to keep the squeegee steady.

10

REMOVE EXCESS STAIN

Wipe off excess stain with a cotton cloth.

11

PULL THE SQUEEGEE ACROSS ALTERNATING LINES

Drag horizontally over every other set of lines, once again using the tape as your guide.

12

STAGGER THE SQUEEGEE

Stagger the placement of the squeegee slightly and drag over the remaining lines.

13
REPEAT THE PROCESS
Repeat dragging the squeegee across alternating sets of lines down the panel until complete. Place the top three teeth of the squeegee in line with the bottom three lines of the previous pull and use them as your guide.

14
REMOVE TAPE
Pull tape off carefully when finished. Allow the finish to dry.

The wicker finish calls for patience and a steady hand, but the results are well worth the effort.

Distressing

✓ STUFF YOU'LL NEED

BASE COAT White Swan satin finish latex paint
GLAZE COAT: White Swan, Basketry, Sophisticated Blue, and Frond Green satin finish latex paints
TOOLS: Drop cloth, paint tray, 2-inch tapered trim brush, plastic container with printed measurements, two 2-inch chip brushes, wood-graining tool, 2-inch and 4-inch plastic trowels
MATERIALS: 120-grit sandpaper, tack cloth, primer, 2-inch low-tack painter's tape, stir sticks, glaze medium, lint-free cotton cloths, paper towels

🕐 TIME TO COMPLETE

Based on a 4×5½-foot armoire
EXPERIENCED: 5 hrs.
HANDY: 6 hrs.
NOVICE: 7 hrs.

◆ BEFORE YOU BEGIN

Remove hardware and mask off any areas you wish to protect with low-tack painter's tape. Prepare the surface by sanding lightly with 120-grit sandpaper and wiping with a tack cloth. It's not necessary to fill the dings, dents, and holes. Prime the entire surface and allow to dry. For additional information, see "Preparing Furniture" on page 155.

White Swan

Basketry

Sophisticated Blue

Frond Green

Add decades to the appearance of furniture by using a distressed finish. For this technique, a wood-graining tool is dragged in a rocking motion across an area glazed in light and dark hues, simulating the real-life wear and tear of aged furniture. It's important that the surface be smooth; any nicks or bumps will cause uneven deposits of glaze. Create various effects by changing the speed with which you rock the tool back and forth and by varying the starting and stopping points. To intensify the aging effect, dip a trowel into undiluted paint and skip it across the surface. Practice with both the wood-graining tool and the trowel on a scrap board until you reach the desired results. For a dramatic, worn look, choose contrasting colors and vary the amount of glaze applied. If desired, add more age by rubbing wood stain over the entire surface with a clean cotton cloth after the piece has dried completely. Distressing can be used on all types of furniture as well as on wainscoting and trim. This look can fit into all types of decorating schemes.

1 APPLY BASE COAT

Use a 2-inch trim brush to apply the White Swan base coat to the outside areas. Paint two coats if necessary. Let dry.

2 APPLY GLAZE TO A SMALL SECTION

Mix 1 part Basketry latex paint and 1 part Sophisticated Blue latex paint to 4 parts glaze medium in a plastic container. Apply to a small area with a 2-inch chip brush. Depending on the size of your project, start with a small amount of glaze. Approximately 1 cup paint to 2 cups glaze was used to treat this cabinet.

DESIGN TIP

PAINT THE INTERIOR
Select any of the colors in the list to paint the interior of the cabinet. The cabinet shown opposite is painted Sophisticated Blue for a brighter overall effect. Apply paint using a 2-inch tapered trim brush. Add a second coat if necessary. Allow to dry before starting the exterior of the cabinet.

3 PULL WOOD-GRAINING TOOL THROUGH

Drag the wood-graining tool over the area you've glazed, rocking it back and forth as you pull. The glaze will stay wet for about 15 minutes, so if you are unhappy with the graining, simply pull the tool through the glaze again. Vary the starting and stopping points of the tool and the dragging speed. After you are satisfied with the results and while the glaze is still wet, turn the tool around and use the comb edge to drag vertically through the glaze.

4 REPEAT THE PROCESS

Repeat Steps 2–3, working one section at a time until completed. Allow to dry.

DESIGN TIP

BRANCH OUT
Try this technique on other items, such as doors that you want to distinguish or furniture pieces that need interest.

4

DECORATIVE TECHNIQUES

DESIGN TIP

INTENSIFY THE EFFECT
Distressing can be taken to any level. Adding a darker glaze to the surface intensifies the effect.

5
BRUSH ON GREEN PAINT
Dip a clean, dry chip brush lightly into the Frond Green latex paint and lightly dab onto a paper towel to help separate the bristles. Drag the brush lightly across the surface in selected areas to build up sections of darker colors.

6
BRUSH ON BLUE PAINT
Repeat Step 5 using Sophisticated Blue latex paint.

7
ALLOW TO DRY
Allow the paint to dry completely.

8
DIP A TROWEL INTO WHITE PAINT
Pour White Swan latex paint into a small paint tray and dip the tip of a plastic trowel into it. Use the 2-inch trowel in small areas and the 4-inch trowel in larger areas.

4

DECORATIVE TECHNIQUES

9

ADD WHITE HIGHLIGHTS WITH TROWEL

Deposit the paint by skipping the trowel lightly across the surface in random areas. Practice skipping the paint on a piece of scrap board before trying it on the furniture. Hold the trowel somewhat flat against the surface to create a more heavily textured look.

10

ALLOW TO DRY

When you've reached the desired results, remove the tape and allow to dry.

Prepare your furniture

Before you add a decorative paint finish to a piece of furniture, you must first prepare the surface. A surface that is properly prepared can make a world of difference to the final paint effect. Plan to spend as much time preparing the piece for a paint finish as you will in applying the finish. Preparation includes repairing surface flaws, sanding, and priming the piece. See page 155 for more information.

4

DECORATIVE TECHNIQUES

Variation

Another technique for distressing furniture includes applying wear and tear to the piece using a set of keys. Sand, prime, and apply the base color. Allow to dry.

1

DISTRESS THE SURFACE

Place a combination of old and new keys onto a large key ring. The different keys will help to vary the texture. Holding the keys by the ring, randomly bounce them against the surface to simulate wear. Make a few scratches with a coin or nail; scrape off some paint by dragging the edge of a knife across a couple of spots. Once the piece is properly distressed, re-sand to simulate more wear.

2

APPLY THE TOP COAT AND SAND THROUGH TO BARE WOOD

Brush on the top coat and let dry. Use contrasting colors for the top coat and base coat. Distress using the same technique as in Step 1. Sand spots through to the first coat to reveal the wood in places that typically receive the heaviest wear, such as edges, corners, and knob and handle areas. Repeat, if desired, with a third color and distress.

Crackling

✓ STUFF YOU'LL NEED

BASE COAT: Hushed White semigloss finish latex paint

TOP COATS: Fresh Peaches, Peas in a Pod, Primrose Garden, and Fresh Heather flat finish latex paints

TOOLS: Plastic container, rubber gloves, drop cloth, 120-grit sandpaper, tack cloth, primer, three 2½-inch trim brushes, 1-inch flat artist's brush

MATERIALS: TSP substitute, stir sticks, crackle medium, wooden knobs approximately 1½ inches wide, water-based polyurethane

🕐 TIME TO COMPLETE

Based on a 2½×3-foot dresser

EXPERIENCED: 4 hrs.

HANDY: 5 hrs.

NOVICE: 6 hrs.

⟳ BEFORE YOU BEGIN

Prepare the surface as directed on page 155. Paint the dresser using the Hushed White base-coat color. Apply two coats if necessary. Allow to dry. If the dresser is already painted white, clean with a TSP substitute, rinse well, and let dry.

Hushed White

Fresh Peaches

Peas in a Pod

Primrose Garden

Fresh Heather

Crackling gives an antiqued, weathered look to furniture, accessories, and trim in just hours. For this effect, crackle medium is applied in between the base coat and top coat. The medium stretches when it gets wet, causing the top coat of paint to crack and exposing the base-coat color underneath. The thickness of the top-coat paint will determine the size of the cracks. A thin layer produces smaller, finer cracks, while a heavier layer results in larger cracks. If you apply the top coat with a roller, cracks will be finer; a brush will give larger cracks. Practice the technique on a piece of scrap board first. This also provides an opportunity to try out different color combinations. Never try to rebrush the top coat; touch-ups will be obvious and will not crack again. If this happens, allow to dry overnight, sand using 120-grit sandpaper, and remove dust with a tack cloth. Recoat with the crackle medium, and allow to dry about two hours before applying the top coat. This finish works well in rooms where a country or rustic look is desired.

1
APPLY CRACKLE MEDIUM
Coat each drawer front with the crackle medium. Brush on thoroughly, then allow to dry for at least two hours.

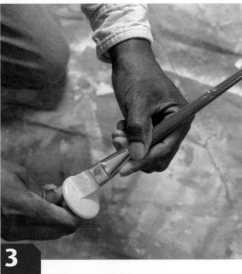

3
PAINT THE KNOBS
Prime and paint unfinished wooden knobs in the colors found in the list and place on different colored drawer fronts. Place as shown in the photo on page 166 or mix and match as you please.

4
FINISH WITH POLYURETHANE
For lasting durability, protect your piece by brushing on two to three coats of a water-based polyurethane after the top coat has dried for at least 24 hours.

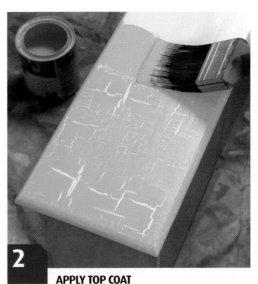

2
APPLY TOP COAT
Working on one drawer at a time, apply a top coat in one of the four colors in the list. With a trim brush, quickly edge the drawer front sides. Paint using vertical brush strokes, moving across the drawer as quickly as possible. This process needs to be started and finished quickly: The finish will begin to crackle within a few minutes. Repeat this process with each drawer front. Allow to dry.

Other applications

Practice this technique on a small piece, such as a picture frame, until you are comfortable with the procedure.

On walls, a crackle finish gives the character of age and makes an effective backdrop for paintings, prints, and photographs.

🎨 DESIGN TIP
MORE DRAWERS, MORE COLORS
If you have more than four drawers, repeat a color, or add in another color, such as a cheerful yellow or darker orange.

📖 WORK SMARTER
ON LARGE SURFACES
If you apply a crackle finish to a large piece, such as a table, it may be easier to control the crackle by dividing the surface into sections, taping them off and working on alternate sections. Let these dry and then very carefully tape off and crackle the remaining sections.

4

DECORATIVE TECHNIQUES

Metallics

✓ STUFF YOU'LL NEED

BASE COAT: Shale Gray satin finish latex paint
METALLIC PAINT: Copper and Carat
TOOLS: Drop cloth, two 1½-inch chip brushes
MATERIALS: Stir sticks, primer, tack cloth, 150-grit sanding block

🕐 TIME TO COMPLETE

Based on the project shown
EXPERIENCED: 3 hrs.
HANDY: 3.5 hrs.
NOVICE: 4 hrs.

↻ BEFORE YOU BEGIN

Prime the item intended to be painted. Be sure to select a primer appropriate for metal surfaces. Allow to dry. Paint the entire piece in the Shale Gray base-coat color. A chip brush works well on intricate surfaces. Allow to dry.

Shale Gray

Copper

Carat

Metallic paints add a satiny shimmer to nearly any surface in just a few hours. Use metallic paint to highlight trim, doors, walls, furniture, accessories, architectural pieces, and flea market finds, such as the treadle sewing machine base shown above. Simply prime the item and apply the base coat first. Add the metallic paint using a chip brush in a stippling up-and-down motion to allow some of the base-coat color to show through. It's a good idea to practice on a piece of scrap board to preview the technique and color selection before starting the project. Metallic paint is also available in spray form. When applying, completely tape off any areas that should be paint-free. Metallic paints also add a dazzling finish to columns, light fixtures, candlesticks, picture frames, drawer knobs, drapery rods and finials, and lamp bases. If the finish is too bright for your taste, tone it down with an umber glaze.

1 **APPLY PAINT TO THE BRUSH**

Shake the Copper metallic paint can. Remove the lid and dip the chip brush into the paint on the lid.

2 **BEGIN PAINTING**

Apply paint to the item using a stippling up-and-down motion. Do not cover the item completely with paint, but allow some of the base-coat color to show through. When you have finished applying the Copper metallic paint, allow it to dry. Wash the chip brush in warm dish detergent and water. For tips on cleaning brushes, see pages 176–177.

GOOD IDEA

TRY A WOODEN SURFACE
If you'd like to give the shiny look of metal to a wooden surface, such as a mirror or picture frame, use a trim brush and apply an even coat of paint. Use a 150-grit sanding block to reveal the base-coat color and some of the raw wood. This will give the piece a rich, aged look. Be sure to switch from a chip brush to a trim brush for solid coverage of the metallic paint.

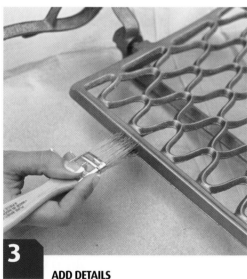

3 **ADD DETAILS**

Add details to the piece using a clean chip brush and Carat metallic paint. Use the same stippling motion, randomly applying the paint here and there to deepen and enrich the color. Allow to dry.

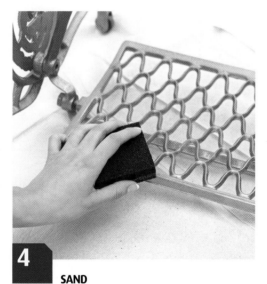

4 **SAND**

If desired, sand the paint to allow more of the base-coat color to show through. The sanding block should be a fairly fine grit, such as 150. Wipe with a tack cloth to remove sanding dust.

4

DECORATIVE TECHNIQUES

Wood-Graining

✓ STUFF YOU'LL NEED

BASE COAT, TOP COAT: Timber Trail semigloss latex paint

TOP COATS: Splish Splash, Celery Leaf, Light Navajo semigloss latex paints

TOOLS: Hammer, nail set, putty knife, pad sander, dust-resistant mask, vacuum cleaner, sponge mop, plastic container, paint tray, standard roller frame with 9-inch roller cover, level with printed ruler or metal yardstick, plastic container with printed measurements, 2-inch chip brush, wood-graining tool, small utility knife, mini roller frame with 6-inch roller cover, mini roller tray

MATERIALS: Latex wood filler, 80-grit sandpaper, glaze medium, 2-inch low-tack painter's tape, 1-inch low-tack painter's tape, stir sticks, white colored pencil, polyurethane

🕐 TIME TO COMPLETE

Based on an 8×8-foot floor

EXPERIENCED: 6 hrs.

HANDY: 7.5 hrs.

NOVICE: 10 hrs.

↻ BEFORE YOU BEGIN

Prepare the floor by filling any cracks wider than ⅛ inch with latex wood filler. Sand lightly with a pad sander using 80-grit sandpaper. Vacuum the floor and damp-mop it to remove all sanding dust. Mask baseboards and trim with low-tack painter's tape. Paint the entire floor in Light Navajo. Paint two coats if necessary. Leave tape on and allow to dry overnight.

I n colonial days, paint was the finish of choice to decorate floors. Today, paint is an even more appropriate selection, especially when faced with specific floor challenges. Plywood floors and wood floors that have been patched with different sizes or types of wood are among the best candidates. Instead of painting a single color, consider the floor a blank canvas and create a decorative paint effect similar to the one shown above. Use this design or draw a design of your own with graph paper and pencil. Tape off the design on the floor and fill in the pattern with color. The finish on the floor shown above uses hues of green, blue, and off-white. After the paint dries, apply a dark glaze mixture using a chip brush. Dragging a wood-graining tool across the wet glaze gives the surface a dimensional, wood-grain effect. To vary the treatment, try different base-coat and top-coat colors to match your home's color scheme, or use natural tones for a realistic wood-grain look. Try changing the center shape to a diamond, or alter the direction of the grain. This finish works well on any flat surface, such as a door, trunk, cabinet, or wainscoting.

Timber Trail

Splish Splash

Celery Leaf

Light Navajo

1
MASK OFF A LARGE SQUARE
Measure and tape off a 4½-foot square. Burnish the edges with a fingernail to ensure a sharp edge when removing tape. Use a standard roller and apply Timber Trail latex paint. Remove tape and allow to dry.

2
MARK THE FLOOR PATTERN
Lay out the floor pattern with a level or metal yardstick. Begin by measuring off a 6-inch border around the perimeter of the square and through the center in both directions.

🔍 **CLOSER LOOK**

THE GREAT COVER-UP
There are several reasons to paint a wood floor, such as covering unsightly repair work or concealing unattractive old varnish. Plus, painting a floor is far less expensive than purchasing carpet.

3
TAPE OFF THE DESIGN
Adhere 1-inch painter's tape to the inside edges of the 6-inch border, leaving a 4-inch reveal. In the center of the design, measure out 4 inches from where the tape crosses and mask off an octagonal shape by simply placing the tape at 45-degree angles. Burnish both sides of the tape with a fingernail to ensure the paint doesn't bleed underneath.

4
CUT OUT THE CENTER TAPE
With a small utility knife, cut out the vertical and horizontal tape in the center, leaving the outline of the octagonal motif.

5 PAINT THE CENTER DESIGN

Paint the center motif and small squares using the 6-inch mini roller and Splish Splash paint.

6 FILL IN THE DESIGN WITH PAINT

Working your way out from the center, use a mini roller to apply the Splish Splash, Celery Leaf, and Light Navajo latex paints: Apply Celery Leaf in the large panels and Light Navajo in the outer border rectangles. Allow to dry.

7 APPLY GLAZE

Mix 1 part Timber Trail to 4 parts glaze in a plastic container. Working with a 2-inch chip brush, paint one section at a time in the direction you wish the grain to appear.

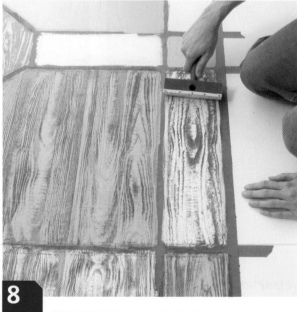

8 PULL THE WOOD-GRAINING TOOL THROUGH THE GLAZE

Drag the wood-graining tool through the wet glaze, rocking back and forth as you pull.

4

DECORATIVE TECHNIQUES

9 BLEND LIGHTLY WITH THE CHIP BRUSH

Without reloading the chip brush, lightly drag it over the surface to blend lines slightly.

10 REPEAT IN EACH SECTION

Apply glaze and drag the wood-graining tool through each section. Continue across the floor working from one side to the other.

11 BLEND EACH NEW SECTION WITH THE CHIP BRUSH

Continue dragging the chip brush over the surface to blend slightly as you go.

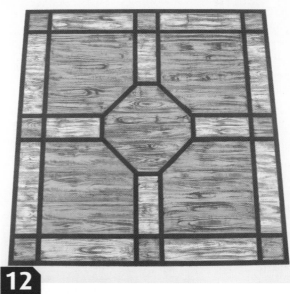

12 ALLOW TO DRY

Remove remaining tape. Allow finish to dry. Apply two to four coats of polyurethane for added durability.

Cleaning up

You're not finished painting until you clean up! This chapter offers advice and tips to make cleanup easier. It starts during painting with wiping up spatters and spills as you go.

After you're finished painting, it's important to follow the steps outlined in the pages that follow to properly care for brushes, rollers, and roller cages so they will be ready for your next painting project. Along with cleaning up painting tools, it's also important to remove paint from your skin and clothes. Store paint in a warm, dry spot so it's ready for touch-ups or another project. Seal cans carefully by removing hardened paint from the rims. Dispose of paint safely using the steps provided or by contacting your local waste management authority.

Chapter 5 highlights

CLEANING BRUSHES
Clean brushes well and they'll last for years. A really smart painter saves the original packaging for storing them too.

176

CLEANING ROLLER COVERS
Is it worth the trouble? Whatever you decide, be sure to wash the cages well.

178

STORAGE AND DISPOSAL
Here's important information on how to store leftover paint for any needed touch-ups and how to dispose of paint you no longer want to keep.

180

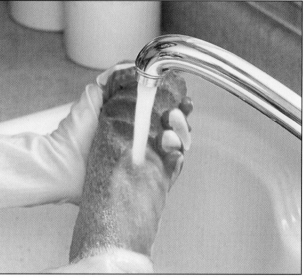

Cleanup may not be exciting, but it's just as important as any other part of the job. Take good care of your tools to ensure the best-looking job possible.

Cleaning brushes

Many professional painters have favorite brushes they have used for years. With proper care, a high-quality brush will see you through multiple paint projects.

Taking care of a brush means never letting paint dry on the bristles, cleaning it completely when a job is finished, and storing it properly, with the bristles in a protective sleeve.

If you have to remove dried paint from a brush, use brush cleaner, which is formulated to remove paint without destroying the brush. Stay away from paint removers; they are too hard on the bristles.

A good brush deserves the care to preserve it. Carefully cleaned, a high-quality brush can last for years.

1 REMOVE AS MUCH PAINT AS POSSIBLE
Brush out as much of the paint as you can onto a newspaper or other disposable surface.

2 RINSE UNDER WARM WATER
Hold the brush under warm running water until the water runs clear.

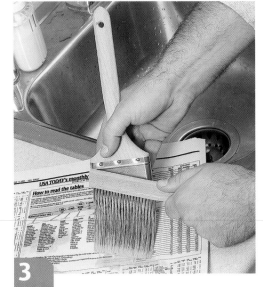

3 REMOVE HARDENED PAINT WITH A COMB
If hardened paint remains against the ferrule, use a wire paint comb to dislodge it.

4 WASH IN DISH DETERGENT
Wash the brush with warm dish detergent or TSP solution, working it up into the ferrule.

5
RINSE UNTIL WATER RUNS CLEAR

Rinse again under clear warm water until all traces of paint have been removed.

6
REMOVE EXCESS WATER

Slap the bristles against your palm several times to remove excess water.

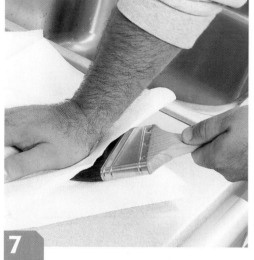

7
BLOT BETWEEN SHEETS OF PAPER TOWEL

Blot the bristles between three to four sheets of paper towel, applying pressure with the heel of your hand.

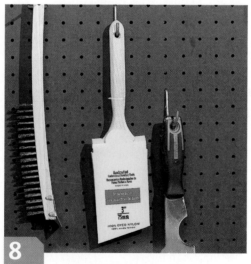

8
STORE IN ORIGINAL HOLDER

Replace the brush in its original cardboard holder. Hang it vertically.

GOOD IDEA

CUSTOM BRUSH COVERS

If the original cardboard brush holder is lost, you can make a replacement cover from shirt cardboard. Fold the cardboard tightly around the ferrule, mark it, then remove and staple together.

GOOD IDEA

SUBSTITUTE

If you don't have a wire paint comb, use a pet comb or an ordinary plastic pocket comb. When it comes to brush care, any attempt at cleaning is better than none.

GOOD IDEA

SOFTEN THEM UP

Brushes that look clean but really aren't can become stiff when they dry. To resoften them, stand the bristles in a solution of 1 tablespoon Murphy's oil soap to 1 gallon of water. Alternatively, soak the bristles in a solution of water and a liquid dishwashing soap that contains alcohol. The alcohol will dissolve any latex residue.

WORK SMARTER

SAFE CLEANING

Many states have banned cleaning brushes in a sink. If yours is one of them, use this three-can process:

- Half fill each of three cans with water (latex paints) or paint thinner (oil-based paints).
- Soak the brush in the first can, moving it up, down, and sideways to remove most of the paint.

- Repeat the process in the second can, and then again in the third.
- Dry the brush by slapping the ferrule on the heel of your hand and pressing the bristles between paper towels.

  Allow the solids to settle. Pour thinner into clean cans for reuse. After the solids have dried, trash them.

5

CLEANING UP

Cleaning roller covers

Roller covers are less expensive than high-quality brushes, don't last as long, and are more difficult to clean. Consequently, the pros often consider them disposable. However, you still may want to clean a high-quality roller cover.

The best way to clean latex paint from a good roller cover is to use a roller spinner. If you don't have a roller spinner, follow the steps shown here. Even the professionals don't try to salvage covers used for oil-based paints.

All of the warnings about disposing of water-thinned latex and solvents down a drain apply to the cleaning of rollers as well. Read "Safe Cleaning" on page 177.

Clean the cage, too. Whether you choose to clean the cover or not, don't forget to clean the roller cage. Removing even hardened paint from the metal cage is relatively simple. Use a wire brush if the paint has hardened.

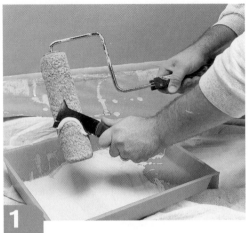

1 REMOVE EXCESS PAINT
Remove as much excess paint as possible by scraping the roller with a handy 10-in-1 tool.

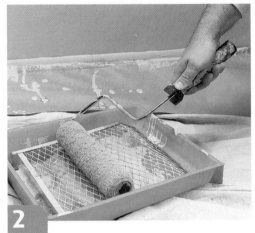

2 USE A PAINT TRAY GRID
Loosen the roller fibers by rolling over a paint tray grid.

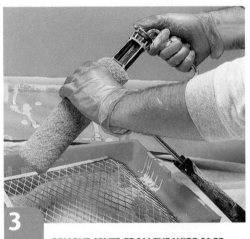

3 REMOVE COVER FROM THE WIRE CAGE
Using rubber gloves, pull the roller cover off the wire cage.

4 RINSE UNDER WARM WATER
Hold the cover under warm running water until the water runs as clear as possible.

Follow these steps to remove latex paint from a roller cover. Clean the cage even if you don't save the cover.

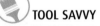 **TOOL SAVVY**

TOO TIRED TO CLEAN?
You can keep a wet roller overnight, either to use the next day, or to delay cleaning.

Put the roller cover in a self-locking, plastic bag and store it in the refrigerator. Or immerse the roller cover in water.

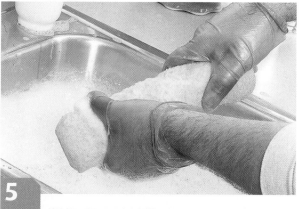

5

WASH USING DISH DETERGENT

Wash the cover in warm water with dish detergent, working the solution into the fibers. (Or soak the cover overnight in a solution of water and a dish detergent that contains alcohol.)

6

RINSE THOROUGHLY

Rinse the detergent solution out of the cover until the water runs clear.

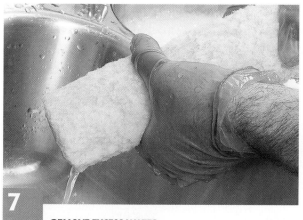

7

REMOVE EXCESS WATER

Squeeze out the excess water by sliding your circled forefinger and thumb down the roller. A roller and brush spinner will get excess water out quickly. You can purchase one at your paint center.

8

STAND ON END TO DRY

Dry and store the wet roller cover by hanging it or standing it on end.

Other cleanups

1

REMOVE PAINT FROM SKIN

Wash your skin in warm soapy water. Scrub resistant spots with a plastic scrub pad.

2

RUB A CLEANING PRODUCT INTO HARDENED PAINT ON CLOTHING

If latex paint has hardened on clothing, rub it with a commercial cleanup product designed to remove hardened paint.

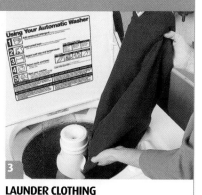

3

LAUNDER CLOTHING

To remove the cleaner and paint residue, run the fabric through a normal wash cycle.

Storage and disposal

Latex paint will store indefinitely, provided two conditions are met:

1. It doesn't freeze.
2. It is sealed in an airtight container.

You can meet the first condition by storing the paint in a warm, dry location. The second requires either transferring the remainder of the paint to a new container or cleaning the rim of all hardened paint, which might interfere with the seal.

Even in an airtight container, the top layer of paint can dry, forming a "skin." It helps to store latex paint cans upside down. This keeps skinning to an absolute minimum and prevents rust from forming on the lip. When you turn the can over to open it, the hardened skin will sink to the bottom of the can.

Save leftover paint for touch-ups and repairs. Stored properly, it can last as long as a coat of paint.

1 TRANSFER PAINT TO A SMALLER CAN
If there is less than 1 quart of paint left, transfer it to a clean, empty quart can.

2 REMOVE PAINT FROM THE RIM
If you are keeping the original can, wipe up paint inside the rim with a small screwdriver wrapped in cloth.

3 TAP THE LID DOWN UNTIL SECURE
Tap the lid down evenly with a block of wood and a hammer.

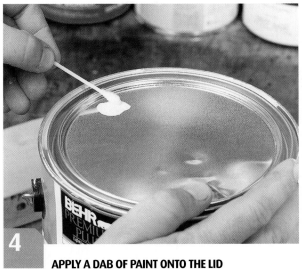

APPLY A DAB OF PAINT ONTO THE LID
Paint a dab of the leftover paint on the lid with a cotton swab. This will help identify the color.

WRITE PERTINENT INFORMATION ON THE LID
Write the paint information on the lid with a permanent black marker.

Disposing of paint and solvents

Liquid paints and solvents can't be tossed out with the household trash—it's against the law. If you have enough left over, consider donating it to a nonprofit organization or charity. Otherwise, you must let the paint and solvents evaporate and solidify and then dispose of them in a manner recommended by your local waste management authority. (Call 800-CLEANUP for information on disposal regulations.) Find a secure place to leave open cans (not in the house or another enclosed space) and leave the lids off until the contents solidify.

To speed up evaporation, especially if you have a significant amount of liquid, add paint hardener, vermiculite, or cat litter to the cans.

To dispose of old latex paint, mix it with paint hardener or vermiculite, let it solidify, then take it to the dump.

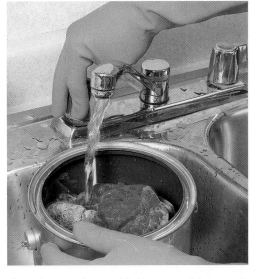

Place solvent rags in a can, fill with water, seal the can, and call your waste management authority for proper disposal.

Patterns

S tripe-and-Stencil Combination (pages 146-150)
- Enlarge each flower 200 percent.
- Make two copies of each flower, three for
Pattern A. Have a copy shop soft-laminate the patterns for
you. Fit as many as you can on one sheet, leaving a 1- or 2-
inch border around each flower so you can cut them apart
easily.
- Purple indicates the first overlay, pink indicates the second
overlay, and green indicates the third overlay.
- Cut out each overlay and stencil using the colors shown
on page 146 or the colors of your choice.
- Use a crafts knife and cut the first overlay shown in
purple. The solid purple and dashed purple lines indicate
where to cut.
- Cut the second and third overlays in the same manner.
- To stencil, put the first overlay on the wall and stencil in
the darkest color (shown on page 150 in orange). Then, line
up the second overlay and stencil in a lighter color (shown on
page 150 in peach). Add the third overlay, which is the
flower center, and stencil in the desired color (shown on
page 150 in green). Embellish with paint pens as desired.

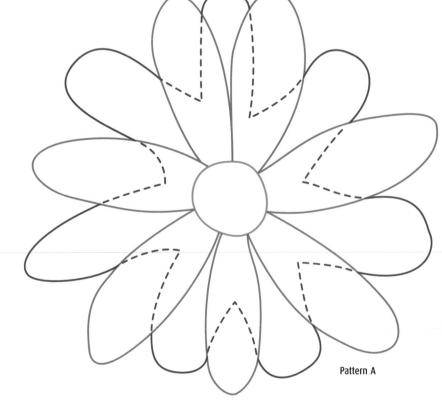

Pattern A

Resources

Special thanks to the following organizations and corporations whose products and advice were instrumental in creating this book:

Behr Process Corporation
3400 W. Segerstrom Avenue
Santa Ana, CA 92704
1-800-854-0133, Ext. 2
www.behrpaint.com

Glidden
1-800-GLIDDEN (454-3336)
www.glidden.com

Dressler Stencil Company
1-888-656-4515
www.dresslerstencils.com

The Stencil Library
+44 (0) 1661 844 844
www.stencil-library.com

Stencil Planet
877-836- 2457
www.stencilplanet.com

Pier 1 Imports

World Market

The listings below include the paint manufacturer, the color name, and the manufacturer's color reference number for the decorative paint projects in Chapter Four.

Fabrics

Page 56: Suede
Suede paint: Ralph Lauren Arrow Wood Marante #SU10

Page 58: Linen
Base coat: Ralph Lauren Stucco White #WW25 semigloss finish latex paint
Glaze coat: Ralph Lauren Alfalfa #NL14

Page 60: Strié
Base coat: Behr Corn Husk Green #400D-4 satin finish latex paint
Glaze coat: Behr Smokey Slate #460E-3 satin finish latex paint
Behr Faux Glaze

Page 64: Grass Cloth
Base coat: Behr Grape Green #400B-5 satin finish latex paint
Glaze coat: Behr Goldenrod Tea #310F-6 satin finish latex paint
Glaze coat: Behr Burley Wood #S-H-700 satin finish latex paint
Behr Faux Glaze
Wall above chair rail: Behr Grape Green #400B-5 satin finish latex paint
Trim: Behr Burley Wood #S-H-700 satin finish latex paint

Page 67: Grass Cloth Variation
Base coat: Behr Velvet Morning #520E-3 satin finish latex paint
Glaze coat: Behr Goldenrod Tea #310F-6 satin finish latex paint
Glaze coat: Behr Harbor #520F-5 satin finish latex paint
Behr Faux Glaze

Page 68: Leather
Base coat: Behr Luster White #W-B-600 semigloss finish latex paint
Glaze coat: Behr Sunset Beige #260F-4 semigloss finish latex paint

Page 71: Leather Variation
(lower left) Base coat: Behr Gondola #3B11-6 semigloss finish latex paint
Glaze coat: Behr Windsor Castle #3A11-4
Behr Faux Glaze
(lower right) Base coat: Behr Seat Salt #780C-1 satin finish latex paint
Glaze coat: Behr Colorado Springs 570D-4 satin finish latex paint
Behr Faux Glaze

Page 72: Antique Leather
Base coat: Ralph Lauren Stadium Red #TH42 satin finish latex paint
Glaze coat: Ralph Lauren Moroccan Red #AL11

Stone

Page 74: Marbleizing
Top coat: Glidden Wood Lily #40YY 83/129 satin finish latex paint
Top coat: Glidden Dark Secret #00NN 05/000 satin finish latex paint
Top coat: Glidden Timber Trail #90YR 10/244 satin finish latex paint
Wall color: Glidden Thundercloud #10GG 26/046 flat finish latex paint
Behr Faux Glaze

Page 77: Marbleizing Variation
Top coat: Glidden Pompeii Clay #60YR 33/287 satin finish latex paint
Top coat: Glidden Costa Mesa #45YY 67/259 satin finish latex paint
Top coat: Glidden Goldstone #00YY 19/261 satin finish latex paint
Behr Faux Glaze

Page 78: Stacked Stones
Base coat: Behr Crème Brulee #360E-1 satin finish latex paint
Stones: Behr Tucson Clay #SND48 Sandwash
Stones: Behr Clay Earth #SND49 Sandwash
Stones: Behr Turtle Shell #SND42 Sandwash

Washes

Page 82: Color Washing
Base coat: Behr Cascade White #W-D-500 satin finish latex paint
Glaze coat: Behr Cinnamon Cherry #S-H-140 satin finish latex paint
Behr Faux Glaze

Page 84: Graduated Color Wash
Base coat: Behr Cottonseed #340E-2 satin finish latex paint
Glaze coat: Behr Salted Ash #2A1-4 satin finish latex paint
Glaze coat: Behr Acorn #290D-6 satin finish latex paint
Glaze coat: Behr Silk Cypress #2A1-3 satin finish latex paint
Glaze coat: Behr Blonde Yellow 2B8-2 satin finish latex paint
Behr Faux Glaze

Page 86: Whitewashing
Top coat: Ralph Lauren Stark White #WW68 semigloss latex paint
Wall above bead board: Ralph Lauren Cowgirl Blue #SS18 satin finish latex paint

Page 88: Double Rolling
Base coat: Behr Wheatfield #3A10-4 satin finish latex paint
Glaze coat: Behr Crepe De Chine #4C5-2 satin finish latex paint
Behr Faux Glaze

Old World:

Page 91: Sponging On
Base coat: Behr Hazelnut Cream #750C-2 satin finish latex paint
Top coat: Behr Crème Brulee #360E-1 satin finish latex paint
Top coat: Behr Raked Leaves #360F-6 satin finish latex paint
Top coat: Behr Dry Sea Grass #360F-4 satin finish latex paint

Page 93: Ragging Off
Base coat: Behr Shimmer satin finish #450E-1 satin finish latex paint
Glaze coat: Behr Southern Breeze #450E-3 satin finish latex paint
Glaze coat: Behr Cottonseed #340E-2 satin finish latex paint
Behr Faux Glaze

Page 95: Ragging On Variation
Base coat: Behr Granite Boulder #790D-4 satin finish latex paint
Glaze coat: Behr Oat Straw #740C-3 satin finish latex paint
Glaze coat: Behr Cottonseed #340E-2 satin finish latex paint
Behr Faux Glaze

Page 96: Aging
Base coat, top coat: Glidden Canvasback #10YY 23/184 flat finish latex paint
Top coat: Glidden Manuscript #40YY 60/103 flat finish latex paint
Top coat: Glidden Clove #80YR 11/244 flat finish latex paint
Behr Faux Glaze

Page 100: Aged Wallpaper
Glaze coat: Ralph Lauren Faux Glaze tinted in Teastain #AG02
Wallpaper: Waverly Country Life #564303 (black)

Page 101: Faded Wallpaper Variation
Glaze coat: Ralph Lauren Faux Glaze tinted in Sunfade #AG01
Wallpaper: Waverly Country Life #564303 (black)

Page 102: Faux Venetian Plaster
Base coat: Glidden Wood Lily #736 40YY 83/129 flat finish latex paint
Top coat: Glidden Seahorse #545 20YY 56/269 flat finish latex paint
Top coat: Glidden Haymarket #532 20YY 44/304 flat finish latex paint
Top coat: Glidden Crème Brulee #414 00YY 26/220 flat finish latex paint

Page 104: Faux Venetian Plaster Variation
Base coat: Glidden Sunshine Coast #40YY 67/196
Top coat: Glidden Sandhill #30YY 55/238
Top coat: Glidden Mojave #30YY 31/205

Page 105: Venetian Plaster
Base coat: Behr New Penny #S-H-210 satin finish latex paint
Plaster coat: Behr Venetian Plaster tinted in Tuscan Villa #VP31

Page 107: Venetian Plaster with Stencil Variation
Base coat: Behr Enchanting Ginger #S-H-320 satin finish latex paint
Plaster coat: Behr Enchanting Ginger #S-H-320 and Behr Cottonseed #340E-2
Stencil: Custom-made

Page 108: Rustic
Base coat: Behr Bavarian Cream #340E-3 satin finish latex paint
Glaze coat: Behr Chestnut Stallion #240D-7 satin finish latex paint
Glaze coat: Behr Wooden Cabin #290F-7 satin finish latex paint
Behr Faux Glaze

Page 112: Texture
Base coat: Behr Honey Tone #360C-3 satin finish latex paint
Glaze coat: Behr Corn Husk Green #400D-4 flat finish latex paint
Behr Smooth texture paint
Behr Faux Glaze

Geometrics

Page 115: Vertical Stripes
Base coat: Behr Cucumber Crush #440C-2 satin finish latex paint
Stripe: Behr Rockwood Jade #440C-3 satin finish latex paint

Page 118: Metallic Horizontal Stripes
Base coat: Ralph Lauren Regent Metallics Stonegate #RM12
Stripe: Ralph Lauren Regent Metallics Turquoise Sea #RM17
Stripe: Ralph Lauren Regent Metallics Ambassador Sterling #RM14

Page 122: Combed Stripe
Base coat: Behr Hazelnut Cream #750C-2 satin finish latex paint
Glaze coat: Behr Romantic Isle #590D-4 satin finish latex paint
Behr Faux Glaze

Page 126: Harlequin Diamonds
Base coat: Behr Timeless Lilac #630C-3 satin finish latex paint
Diamonds: Behr Ruffled Iris #630D-4 satin finish latex paint

Page 130: Blocks
Base coat: Behr Bright Citrus 240A-3 satin finish latex paint
Color Block: Behr Marmalade 240B-4 satin finish latex paint
Color Block: Behr Torchlight #290B-5 satin finish latex paint
Color Block: Behr Fiery Red #180B-6 satin finish latex paint
Color Block: Behr Fruit Shake #180B-4 satin finish latex paint
Color Block: Behr Cheerful Hue #330B-4 satin finish latex paint

Stenciling

Page 133: Allover Stenciling
Base coat: Ralph Lauren Aged Mint #IB25 satin finish latex paint
Stencil coat: Ralph Lauren Capri #GH77 satin finish latex paint
Stencil coat: Ralph Lauren Big Sur Blue #IB33 satin finish latex paint
Stencil: Florentine Damask Medium #564M, Dressler Stencil Company,
888-656-4515 or www.dresslerstencils.com

Page 136: Random Stenciling
Base coat: Glidden Spruce Tint #50GG 42/096 satin finish latex paint
Top coat: Glidden Bird's Nest #90YR 10/151 satin finish latex paint
Stencil: Cherry Blossom #DR2, The Stencil Library, +44 (0) 1661 844 844 or
www.stencil-library.com

Page 138: Embossed Stenciling
Base coat: Glidden Overcast #10BG 38/044 flat finish latex paint
Glaze coat: Glidden Manuscript #40YY 60/103 flat finish latex paint
Behr Faux Glaze
Stencils: Arabian Border #10126 and Far Eastern Flower #10129, Stencil Planet,
877-836- 2457 or www.stencilplanet.com

Kid's Rooms

Page 142: Denim
Base coat: Ralph Lauren Cowgirl Blue #SS18 semigloss finish latex paint
Glaze coat: Ralph Lauren Blue Print #ID06
Above chair rail: Ralph Lauren Mission Wildflower #GH138 satin finish latex paint

Page 146: Stripe-and-Stencil Combination
Base coat: Behr Coastal Mist #520E-1 satin finish latex paint
Stripe: Behr Hushed White #W-F-710 semigloss finish latex paint
Stencil coat: Behr Fresh Heather #650A-3 satin finish latex paint
Stencil coat: Behr Primrose Garden #130B-4 satin finish latex paint
Stencil coat: Behr Fresh Peaches #260C-3 satin finish latex paint
Stencil coat: Behr Mango Madness #S-G-280 satin finish latex paint
Stencil coat: Behr Peas in a Pod #430B-4 satin finish latex paint
Rustoleum American Accents Decorative Paint Pens in Petal Pink, Lilac, and
White satin finishes

Page 151: Clouds
Base coat: Ralph Lauren Seasport #SS51 satin finish latex paint
Clouds: Ralph Lauren Water Lily #SS02 satin finish latex paint
Clouds: Ralph Lauren Coastal Blue #SS33 satin finish latex paint
The Woolie Cloud Kit or The Woolie Decorative Painting Kit
Ralph Lauren Decorator's Glaze

Furniture & More

Page 154: Chalkboard Paint
Primer: Ralph Lauren Deep Base Primer tinted to match Ralph Lauren Hunting
Coat Red #TH43
Base coat: Ralph Lauren Hunting Coat Red #TH43 semigloss latex paint
Rustoleum Chalk Board Paint
Wall color: Ralph Lauren Big Sur Blue #IB33 satin finish latex paint

Page 157: Wicker
Base coat: Glidden Costa Mesa #45YY 67/259 semigloss finish latex paint
MinWax Golden Oak Gel Stain

Page 162: Distressing
Cabinet interior: Glidden Sophisticated Blue #1509 30BB 46/142 satin finish
latex paint
Base coat: Glidden White Swan #60YY 83/062 satin finish latex paint
Glaze coat: Glidden Basketry #20YY 31/205 satin finish latex paint
Glaze coat: Glidden Sophisticated Blue #30BB 46/142 satin finish latex paint
Glaze coat: Glidden Frond Green #50GY 51/141 satin finish latex paint
Behr Faux Glaze

Page 166: Crackling
Base coat: Behr Hushed White #W-F-710 semigloss finish latex paint
Top coat: Behr Fresh Peaches #260C-3 semigloss finish latex paint
Top coat: Behr Peas in a Pod #430B-4 semigloss finish latex paint
Top coat: Behr Primrose Garden #130B-4 semigloss finish latex paint
Top coat: Behr Fresh Heather #650A-3 semigloss finish latex paint
Primer: Behr All-Purpose Primer
Behr Crackle Medium
Behr Crystal Clear Water-Based Polyurethane #780

Page 168: Metallics
Base coat: Behr Shale Gray #540F-4 satin finish latex paint
Behr Premium Plus with Style Metallic Copper #742
Behr Premium Plus with Style Metallic 14 Carat #741
Behr Primer

Page 170: Wood-graining
Base coat, top coat: Glidden Timber Trail #90YR 10/244 semigloss latex paint
Top coat: Glidden Light Navajo #40YY 76/112 semigloss latex paint
Top coat: Glidden Splish Splash #90GG 49/159 semigloss latex paint
Top coat: Glidden Celery Leaf #90YY 57/543 semigloss latex paint
Behr Faux Glaze

Index

INDEX

Toolbox essentials: nuts-and-bolts books for do-it-yourself success.

Save money, get great results, and take the guesswork out of home improvement projects with a growing library of step-by-step books from the experts at The Home Depot.®

Packed with lots of projects and practical tips, these books help you design, remodel, decorate, and repair your home or garden. Easy-to-follow, step-by-step instructions and colorful photographs ensure success. Projects even estimate time, skills, materials needed, and tools required.

**You can do it.
We can help.**℠

Shahjahan Ali
Nile, IL

Thomas Barton
Gurnee, IL

Nigel D. Brown
Vinings, GA

Bob Canty
Ingleside, IL

Jennifer M. Cook
Chicago, IL

Tino Fortes
Vinings, GA

Allen Haack
Geneva, IL

Steven R. Hoffman
Downers Grove, IL

Victor A. Jimenez
Chicago, IL

Cristina Kida
Duluth, GA

Many thanks to
the employees of
The Home Depot® whose
"wisdom of the aisles"
has made *Decorative
Painting 1-2-3®* the most
useful book of its kind.

Jennifer O. Lawrence
Atlanta, GA

Clint Moss
Alpharetta, GA

Norma S. Opiela
Schaumburg, IL

Edward W. Psioda
Gurnee, IL

Jeffrey Schroeder
Lawrenceville, GA

Lester A. Scott
Lawrenceville, GA

Tom Thompson
Brookwood, GA

Zac Villano
Glenview, IL

Bonnie Wallace
Marietta, GA

Tom Sattler
Atlanta, GA